BE REAL IN A
THE BEAUTIFUL

ECHOES OF EXPRESSION

Edited By Briony Kearney

First published in Great Britain in 2025 by:

Young Writers
Remus House
Coltsfoot Drive
Peterborough
PE2 9BF
Telephone: 01733 890066
Website: www.youngwriters.co.uk

All Rights Reserved
Book Design by Ashley Janson
© Copyright Contributors 2024
Softback ISBN 978-1-83685-068-7
Printed and bound in the UK by BookPrintingUK
Website: www.bookprintinguk.com
YB0621B

Foreword

Since 1991, here at Young Writers we have celebrated the awesome power of creative writing, especially in young adults where it can serve as a vital method of expressing their emotions and views about the world around them. In every poem we see the effort and thought that each student published in this book has put into their work and by creating this anthology we hope to encourage them further with the ultimate goal of sparking a life-long love of writing.

Our latest competition for secondary school students, The Beautiful Truth, asked young writers to consider what their truth is, what's important to them, and how to express that using the power of words. We wanted to give them a voice, the chance to express themselves freely and honestly, something which is so important for these young adults to feel confident and listened to. They could give an opinion, highlight an issue, consider a dilemma, impart advice or simply write about something they love. There were no restrictions on style or subject so you will find an anthology brimming with a variety of poetic styles and topics. We hope you find it as absorbing as we have.

We encourage young writers to express themselves and address subjects that matter to them, which sometimes means writing about sensitive or contentious topics. If you have been affected by any issues raised in this book, details on where to find help can be found at
www.youngwriters.co.uk/info/other/contact-lines

Contents

Independent Entrants

Tigerlily (12) — 1

Ashford School, Ashford

Elisabeth Hinsley (12) — 2
Sara Alhajali — 4
F Sadler — 5
F Hanover (11) — 6
Charlotte Ellaway (11) — 7
Avery Kuijpers — 8
William Morris — 9
Oliver Woolnough — 10
Josiah Dzikunu (11) — 11

Buckler's Mead Academy, Yeovil

Greta Samori (12) — 12
Samuel Potten (15) — 14
Cerys Llewellyn (14) — 15
Poppy Stickley (12) — 16
Lilly Moss (13) — 17
Layton Thomas (13) — 18

Cantell School, Bassett

Balqiisa Osman (13) — 19
Pip Seely-Hall (13) — 20
Gleb Vorobev — 21
James Haslehurst — 22
Katharina H — 23

Chiltern Academy, Luton

Alishbah Iqbal (15) — 24
Gurneet Kaur (13) — 25

Ruby Shuker (11) — 26
Faryaal Zarrar (11) — 27

Claires Court School, Maidenhead

Harrison McNamee (13) — 28
Varan Prem Anand (13) — 30
George Lomas (13) — 32
Vihaan Tailor (13) — 33
Toby Price (13) — 34
Ollie Williamson (13) — 36
Louis Manley (12) — 37
Harry Notton-Brown (12) — 38
William Gowers (11) — 39
Ethan Nation (14) — 40
Fred Luke (13) — 41
Oscar Brown (11) — 42
Robert O'Hagan (12) — 43
Ewan Densley (11) — 44
Rory Macmillan (11) — 45
Sebastian Bose (13) — 46
Aarav Singh (12) — 47
Jack Morrissey (12) — 48
Jake Milborrow (11) — 49
Dylan Moore (12) — 50
Freddie Carpenter (13) — 51
Finlay Milner (13) — 52
Thomas Kohler (12) — 53
Barnaby Morgan (12) — 54

Clydeview Academy, Gourock

Glenn McKerracher (13) — 55
Ruaridh McClure (13) — 56
Katie Dunnet — 58
Finley Buchan — 60

Xander Young (13)	61
Amy MacLellan	62
Flynn McLellan (13)	63
Mikey Cardona	64
Katie Sullivan (13)	65
Ellie Stewart (13)	66

Hereford Cathedral School, Hereford

Ruqaya El (15)	67
Anna Price (16)	68
Astrid Westerlund (14)	70
Sylvie Hart (16)	72
Milly Clarke (11)	73
Kyro Hanna (16)	74
Ellen Carroll (15)	76
Theo Gerrand (15)	77
Sian Howells (12)	78
Naiya Davidson (15)	79
Annabelle Jackson (12)	80
Matilda Driver (11)	81
Laura Dean (15)	82
Martha Trafford-Roberts	84
Rowan McIntyre (11)	86
Gelliert Thacker-Vuts (13)	88
Grace Clokie (13)	90
Honor Watts (15)	92
Finlay Webb (11)	93
Leonidas Morphis (15)	94
Luke Williamson (11)	95
Romilly Elliott (11)	96
Sophia O'Leary	97
Avitej Singh	98
Ruth Mattos (16)	100
Alice Morris Dawson (13)	101
George Martin (15)	102
Huw Pritchard (16)	103
Owain Howells (15)	104
Matilda Judd (14)	105
Edward White (11)	106
Daisy Fleetwood (14)	107
George Brown (11)	108
Daisy Hall (13)	109
Jacob Denslow (14)	110
Olive York Moore (12)	111
Isla Storey (12)	112
Evie Prowse (11)	113
Reuben Alcott (15)	114
Bethany Hodgson-Hutton (13)	115
Jack Evans (11)	116
Annie Wall (13)	117
Lucy Olivia Forker (12)	118
Tom Norman (13)	119
Charlotte Middleton (13)	120
Alice Blandford (13)	121
Maisie Fenner (14)	122
Fearn Middleton (13)	123
Issy North (15)	124
Stanley McIntyre (13)	125
Phoebe Matthews (16)	126
Evie Jones (11)	127
Charlie Fowler (12)	128
Izzy Early (12)	129
Elodie Alcott (13)	130
Artie Jackson (11)	131
Emilia John (12)	132
Clara West (13)	133
Esme Yorke (16)	134
Archie Gladwyn (11)	135
Mary Connop (15)	136
Ollie Yates (15)	137
Evelyn Davies (13)	138
Ashley Wilson (12)	139
Mimi Boniface (15)	140
Jack Jones (15)	141
Monty Harrison (12)	142
Daimen James (13)	143
Toby Baxter (12)	144
Emily Driver (15)	145
Arabella Clark (15)	146
William Ingmire (12)	147
Mary Wardle (11)	148
Mylo Verrall-Bhasin (12)	149
Toby Whitaker (12)	150
Glasha Connolly (13)	151
Harry Buchanan (12)	152

Lola Wyatt (12)	153
Eleanor Huxtable (11)	154
Martha Powell (12)	155
Barnaby West (11)	156
George Hinton (12)	157
Hunter Martin (12)	158
Matthew Hughes (13)	159
Ali Elrefaiy (13)	160
Harry Crawford (12)	161
Zachary Pepper-Wilby (12)	162
Robin Hughes (15)	163

Highfields School, Matlock

Moon Carr (18)	164
Leila Brett (13)	166
Lexi Robinson (13)	167
Immy Rifkin (13)	168
Daniel Jellis (12)	169

Laleham Gap School, Ramsgate

Dylan James (17)	170
Henry Hoile (16)	172
Thurston Miles (16)	173

Monkton Combe Senior School, Monkton Combe

Mima James (14)	174
Anouk Chioke (14)	176
Faith Karamura (14)	178
Amber Ashman	180
Ashley Fai	182
Rufus Difazio (14)	184
Walter Wheeler	186
Ana Champion (14)	187
Jayden Swanston (15)	188

New College Leicester, Leicester

Denis Rimeikis (13)	189
Harmony Uwujare (14)	190
Yannis Dorobantu (13)	192
Ivie Saddler (13)	193

Onyx Onyekwere (11)	194
Hafsat Sulaiman (14)	195
Rhuben Glover (13)	196
Travaee Pearson (11)	197
Amelia Pitijeva (13)	198
Janiah Semedo (11)	199
Joseph Mulroy (12)	200
Paulina Jokubauskyte (12)	201
Amira Moon (13)	202
Hollie Wain McCabe (13)	203
Hollie Hirons (11)	204
Phoebe Coles (11)	205
Fidelis Appiah (12)	206
Mariam Shamsaddin (11)	207
Caden Flattley (13)	208
Honya Fuad (13)	209
Freddie Burdett (14)	210

Penrice Academy, St Austell

Kaitlyn Doyle (11)	211
Caja Dowrick (11)	212
Seren Thompson (11)	214
Charlie Chesterfield (11)	215
Keyaan Patel (11)	216
Mollie Lee Baxter (11)	217

Pinderfields Hospital PRU, Wrenthorpe

R Stephenson (14)	218
S Ali	220
F McCulloch	222

Slemish College, Ballymena

Janna Greer (15)	223
Marta Ossowska (14)	224
Joel Hagan (13)	226
Paulina Ossowska (12)	227

The Elland Academy, Leeds

Tayyab (11)	228
Benji Remmer (12)	229
Ellis Rockliffe (13)	230

Thomas Telford School, Telford

Florence Morris (13)	231
Eva Ligori (11)	232
Kaitlan Astill-Evans (13)	233
Luis Reeves (12)	234
Seerat Maan (11)	235
Kasper Johnson (13)	236

Townley Grammar School For Girls, Bexleyheath

Jessica Shokanbi (11)	237
Isabella French-Compagnoni (15)	238
Rosanna McNeil (17)	241
Eva Matthew (15)	242
Fire Depiver (11)	244
Michelle Fayoyin (15)	246
Comfort Adeyinka (16)	248
Victoria Esther Gilgal-Sale (11)	250
Iris Njomgang (11)	252
Harleen Mann (11)	254
Safiya Marbin (11)	256
Asmitha Cathiskanthan (12)	257
Momore Sina-Atanda (12)	258
Joanna Elegbede (11)	259
Emilie King (11)	260
Anayah Springer (12)	261

Tudor Hall School, Banbury

Emma Wang (12)	262
Olivia Ormazabal (10)	265
Maisie Gross (12)	266

THE POEMS

Dogs

Dogs are like frogs,
They hop through the fields,
Pouncing off furniture,
As they yield.

Dogs are like cats,
Sweet but ambitious,
If they're not trained properly,
They can be vicious.

Dogs are like birds,
They like their freebies,
Taking flight in the air,
Before landing back down ungracefully.

Dogs are like horses,
They need their nutrition,
And go nuts,
For their sweet treat addiction.

Tigerlily (12)

What Magic Feels Like

In my dreams, I see myself
My name emblazoned on a thick novel
A pen in my hand.

Worlds are spilling from my pen
Like ink on a page
Like past becoming present.

Turning into the minds of other people
Sharing thoughts and feelings
Sharing hopes and dreams.

I see faraway places
Magical palaces
All coming alive before my two eyes

Magic and myths
Talking and walking animals
A portal within the pages of a book
I can control the wind
I can fly into countless galaxies
I can create anything my mind wishes for

I can soar on clouds and ride the waves
I can leap between the branches of the Tree of Life
And I can plummet down a deep pit to Hell.

These worlds are my being
I cannot imagine myself without ink on my face
Cheeks creased from falling asleep reading.

When my emotions are out of control
Threads out of reach
Spiralling through a never-ending web

I simply take up my pen
Place it on a clear, unmarked page
And dive into my personal cave of wonders

And that
Is what magic feels like.

Elisabeth Hinsley (12)
Ashford School, Ashford

Everything Is Possible

I believe that dreaming, ambition and hope are the keys to success
Everyone has unique dreams and goals, so they said
Never back down, never give up and believe in yourself
Some people dream big, some dream small
But every dream needs working hard for
Some people want to be footballers, some want to be runners
Some want to make the Olympics while others want to win the Euros
Some people want to be artists, some people want to be musicians
Some people want to blast off into space while others dive deep into the oceans
Some people want to be doctors and some want to be architects
But most importantly, you have to remember that everything is possible if you put your mind to it
If you ever fall down to the ground, rise up with more determination to fulfil it
Failure is the way to success and trying hard is the key
If anyone brings you down or says you can't do something, remember it's just jealousy
So don't be afraid to dream and hope, because everything is possible if you slowly climb up the slope.

Sara Alhajali
Ashford School, Ashford

Make Your Mark

It starts off all happy - with no care in the world,
It doesn't always feel like that, sometimes the pages fold.

Although the middle may seem hard, sad or worrying,
There may be a time - a conflict, as such, may change your day, a wonderful day.
But there is still more to come, the pages keep turning.

And then the end closes near.
You speak and speak - but no one responds;
Use your voice while people can hear you.

We all have a voice, but are all different inside:
Like apples, melons, oranges, even trees, we are all different in most ways but except we are all human, all together as one.
So use your voice and be remembered, if not for your voice, for your thoughts.

F Sadler
Ashford School, Ashford

The Seabirds' Dreams

Like a wave amidst the sea,
The seabirds sing and dance and twirl,
They've feelings just like me.

Spinning up and spinning down,
Pirouetting through the sky,
Up until the evening sunshine sank low, began to die.

The seabirds' dreams were vivid
They dreamt of hope and grace,
They wished away their problems,
All the things they had to face.

And that night, they saw their problems
As insubstantial, silly worries,
They sang their songs into the clouds,
And disappeared in flurries.

So we could learn a thing or two
From those small seabirds that once flew,
That flew with ease throughout the sky,
Until the sky turned red with sunset and the day began to die.

F Hanover (11)
Ashford School, Ashford

Change

The world needs to change,
The only thing we hear about is war,
Violence and discrimination,
It doesn't only happen in some places,
It happens all across the nation.

The world needs to change,
When will it end?
When will the shouts and cries
Stop being covered up with pathetic lies?
When will it become the truth?
When will people be accepted for who they are,
Whether they like hairbrushes,
Nature or pink cars?
It shouldn't be a problem of where people come from,
What they wear,
What they like to eat and what they do on their weekend,
Because we are all equal, and all it starts with is change.

Charlotte Ellaway (11)
Ashford School, Ashford

I Want To Be

I want to be a pharmacist, a hard-working person
Who helps people to get their lives back.

I want to be a pharmacist who is respectful and
Kind towards others.

I want to be a pharmacist, who fills the capsules,
Packages the capsules and gives the capsules.

I want to be a pharmacist, who gets the job done
And in a careful manner.

I want to be a pharmacist because I don't want to
See the unpleasant scenes.

I want to be a pharmacist who helps save lives.

I want to be a pharmacist and I think you should
Consider it too.

Avery Kuijpers
Ashford School, Ashford

Life

Life is a weird and wonderful thing,
It is mostly a treasured possession,
Some love it, some hate it,
But where would we be without it?

Life is not endless, at some point,
Death will catch up with you,
Usually, people fear that day,
But some look forward to it.

Some people believe that you either go to heaven (or hell),
Others say that you live again.
Some believe that you could possibly gain enlightenment,
Others say that you float around in nothingness.

What people agree on, however,
Is that life is too short,
Enjoy it whilst you can,
And remember, happiness cannot be bought.

William Morris
Ashford School, Ashford

Football

I believe every kick is different,
from scoring to giving it a go,
even if you don't think you can do,
never say never, don't say no,
through the sun and rain,
remember mistakes are life,
it's all in the game,
you win, lose and draw as a team,
we are all not exactly the same,
it's not all bad though,
you can have fun, don't forget that,
football is a game
that you can play no matter what,
remember one thing,
we are all not the same.

Oliver Woolnough
Ashford School, Ashford

Diversity

As the undulating sun glistens upon the heather.
Bringing serenity and prosperity with day.
May lives be subjugated with leisure.
'Til the morn', man's corpse lay.
Yes, 'til the morn', man's corpse lay.

No matter what hue or complexion man has: mixed race, black or white.
May empathy subdue all men.
May ruin encapsulate those who take plight.
May God bless all, Amen.
Yes, may God bless all, Amen.

Josiah Dzikunu (11)
Ashford School, Ashford

Poppies Growing

Poppies growing, more men dying,
all the Nazis multiplying,
Hitler leading, killing Jews,
so much more than just abuse!

Poppies growing, families crying,
all the people denying and dying,
it's not okay, this needs to stop,
it's not okay for Jews to get shot!

Poppies growing, more and more bombing,
the population drastically dropping,
this is getting out of hand,
where is the saviour we are longing?

Poppies growing, V-Day is here,
Germans surrender,
finally, Jews are back at their centre,
bombing gone, celebrations begin,
what else could we do with this big win?

Poppies growing, tombs getting dug,
this wouldn't have been the fate they picked,
families crying, wanting to roll the die,
saving the ones they love,
instead of them turning into a dove...
Poppies growing, 80 years from that day,
but we still remember where they lay,

we will never forget all they did,
as they gave a good life to our kids,
but most importantly, we will never forget what the poppies hid...

Greta Samori (12)
Buckler's Mead Academy, Yeovil

Death Of A Companionship

She messaged me at nine
My sorrows heaped at that time.
I sat as she got the words down
And I couldn't help but frown.
For reasons I can't understand
But was it always so damned?
She said we must part
That emptied my heart.
We are told all love must pass
But why so fast?
I am one of few who believe
There must be more to love
Than what those conceive.
And now I fight for the days
For when I may escape this maze.
And there again...
I remember as the words stopped
My sorrows came to flop.

And then I remembered the time
She messaged me at nine.

Samuel Potten (15)
Buckler's Mead Academy, Yeovil

Mental Health Isn't A Game

Students say school is bad,
But they don't explain why they're so mad,
They feel like they're not there,
Unless it's for a dare.

Boys get told not to be sad,
So instead they are bad,
It's so sad,
Everyone should have the freedom that they had.

Mental health isn't just a game,
That teachers think they can tame,
With punishments and blame,
As the new therapist asks, "What's your name?"

Children should be heard,
And not just feel like a bird,
Chirping so loud but no one can hear a sound.

Cerys Llewellyn (14)
Buckler's Mead Academy, Yeovil

Are You Observant?

I ndependent beautiful minds create wonderful images in our head

L earning new ways to represent our work we've read

O utstanding stories, poems, and scripts

V arious vocabulary that sometimes makes our mouths trip

E xcellent formats and handwriting

P erfect punctuation for bookmaking

O rganised story structures that create a pretty picture

E xcellent articles are made

M aybe you even noticed down the side at the start of each sentence

S pells I love poems...

Poppy Stickley (12)
Buckler's Mead Academy, Yeovil

The Happiness Of Life

Outside is for having fun
You go home to greet your mum
Not everyone is the same
That is what makes life a game
No matter how big, small or different you may be
People need to be set free
The happiness of life can make you jolly or sad
Which can make people feel bad
Everyone has their ways
That is what makes life okay
Now that this poem is nearly done
Kids' minds have just begun
The happiness of life can be great
Or it can be filled with hate.

Lilly Moss (13)
Buckler's Mead Academy, Yeovil

Unstoppable

Some people live in a world that is fake,
They think it's all easy, a piece of cake,
But reality is, life's cruel and unjust,
But a thing that'll save you is a little bit of trust,
And if there's one thing I've learnt from being gay,
Is that cruelty is never going to pay,
So next time you think it's too late to land,
Remember this, you can hold out a hand,
And reach new heights you thought were impossible,
You'll be a hero, unstoppable.

Layton Thomas (13)
Buckler's Mead Academy, Yeovil

Winter

In winter's frozen clutch,
Shadows stretch like weary hands.
A biting frost slips through my coat,
Each breath, a ghost lingers -
A reminder that warmth has gone astray.

The trees stand as quiet witnesses,
Their branches bare like forgotten promises;
Each leaf, a story snatched by the gale,
Drifting further into the void of silence.

Footsteps crunch on the icebound paths,
Their echoes swallowed by the night.
A distant laugh, once vibrant and clear,
Now muffled and lost like whispers of smoke
Vanishing into the chill of despair.

The sun hides beneath a shroud of clouds.
Its light a flicker, dim and uncertain.
Nights stretch endlessly...
Each chapter, steeped in a shadow
Haunted by echoes turned into sighs.

Windows frost like forgotten dreams,
Each breath, inside a fleeting sigh.
I wonder through the silent expanse,
A solitary figure wrapped in twilight,
Yearning for warmth that lingers beyond reach.

Balqiisa Osman (13)
Cantell School, Bassett

Hello Summer, Goodbye Summer

Summer starts when you've crossed off all the days in May,
When jumpers go back to hiding in the attic and shorts and cotton dresses come out of hibernation,
When you go for your first trip to the beach,
When the first cherry blossom gets tangled in the breeze.

And summer passes slowly with the scent of chlorine in your hair,
With lemonade and grape squash,
With flip-flop blisters between your toes,
With rushes through the airport,
With suntan turned to sunburn.

But summer ends when you've crossed off all the days in August,
When the cotton dresses fade,
When you clean the sand from the bottom of your bag,
When the first brown leaf falls,
When you buy a stiff new pair of school shoes.
And just like that, summer ends.
Like an ice lolly: drip, drip, drip and then it's gone.

Pip Seely-Hall (13)
Cantell School, Bassett

Baa, Baa, No Sheep

Baa, baa, black sheep, do you have any wool?
We gave you food water and
All we need is you to stay with others
Even if it might be cramped and without your mother

And don't dare say you have nothing left to give
Because we will make sure you cease to live
We'll make you eat extra, if it comes down to that
To ensure your pie doesn't fall flat

But don't you worry, we'll make sure
We get a good price for your fur
Even if the price is a little much
We'll just lie and say you weren't trapped in a hutch

So sleep tight, little sheep, to make that wool
Or we will simply make our stomachs full.

Gleb Vorobev
Cantell School, Bassett

Blossoms Of Hope

New life awakens with a thankful cheer,
Plants unfurling, reaching to the sky.
Birdsong fills the morning air, a chorus of celebration,
As the world beats back winter's icy grip.
Drops of rain meet the ground, sharing secrets with the soil.
Signs of life emerge, a promise of warmer days.

Meanwhile, in the stillness of dawn,
The scent of blossom lingers on.
A reminder that no matter what,
Spring always returns with a smile.

James Haslehurst
Cantell School, Bassett

Winter

The days grow sleepily shorter
The world is reduced to dirty white
Becomes closed off, warping
Into the bleakest wonderland

Some say it's magical
But I pine for the summer
A memory now fading
Obscured by falling snow

Ice like cracked glass
Mirroring my soul
Beautiful, broken
Waiting to thaw.

Katharina H
Cantell School, Bassett

How?

How can I express myself,
when all I feel is nothing?
With writing,
we have to be willing to press the pen against the paper,
hoping to see what parts of ourselves are willing to tell their stories.
With talking,
we have to be willing to sit down with the parts of our souls,
waiting to be heard,
waiting to be listened to,
waiting to be mocked.
How can I express myself,
when I don't even know myself?
How can I talk about myself,
when I can't even find where I am?
Hoping and crying and screaming,
it's a challenge, isn't it?
All the noise in my head,
all the hate in my head,
all the anger in my head,
hoping and begging for it to stop,
crying and screaming. It's all a dream,
or is it?

Alishbah Iqbal (15)
Chiltern Academy, Luton

Disguise

In this world of screens and digital disguise,
Where truth is veiled by countless blinds,
I seek the core within my heart so true,
A beacon glowing in a shimmering sea of blue.

Beneath the filters, masks, and AI's gaze,
I cling to fragments of my beloved yesterdays,
When laughter echoed through the woods so green,
And joy was found in simple, soulful scenes.

ChatGPT and Gemini are friends.
What about those I befriend?
Living life with AI
Living in hell.

For moments that are peaceful
There is opposition to it.
In this world of screens and digital disguise,
Where truth is veiled by countless blinds,
I seek the core within my heart so true.
Where is my family?
Why is it you?

Gurneet Kaur (13)
Chiltern Academy, Luton

The Pages Turned

The pages turned
The girl stepped in
Her stomach churned
Deep down within
She felt her freedom
Slip away
She was captured
Someone's prey
She gripped the bars
And pulled them tight
The bars, they thinned
That wasn't right
The floor gave out
She fell and fell
And gave a shout
Beneath her, hell
She focused on
The novel's name
And to her rescue
Memory came
The walls came back
She shut the book
But do you dare
To take a look?

Ruby Shuker (11)
Chiltern Academy, Luton

Fake Friends

You treat them as if
They have a heart like yours
But not everyone can be
As soft and as tender as you
You don't see
The person they are
You see the person
They have the potential to be
You give and give 'til
They have taken everything
Out of you and leave
You empty.

Faryaal Zarrar (11)
Chiltern Academy, Luton

Innocent Lives Gone In A Second

Living, breathing, dying, hunting.
Bringing people to their graves.
Chasing, shrieking, pouncing, killing.
Dragging bodies to its dark cave.

Running, screaming, falling, dying.
Innocent souls struck down again.
Biting, scratching, tearing, haunting.
More shall join its everlasting pain.

Shouting, killing, lying, hiding.
They are monsters alive.
Capturing, killing, crying, flying.
Not letting them live their lives.

Begging, crying, sighing, praying.
More pulled to their deaths.
Begging, crying, praying, dying.
Unknowingly, they take their final breath.

Their monstrosity knows no bounds.
The filthy dictator with no care for the cost.
Sending more to the death grounds.
Nothing good came from the Holocaust.

Six million dead.
Killed by Nazis.
It fills us with dread.
Across the seas.

Genocide must end.
Those people questioned.
Our past we must mend.
It causes innocent lives to be gone in a second.

Harrison McNamee (13)
Claires Court School, Maidenhead

One's Gone Mad

One's gone mad.
One's gone mad.

One's throat is slit
like an animal struck by
the tiger.

One person is awake
whilst another is in
pain as if he got bitten
by a snake.

One person's organs
are robbed, sold to
another gone mad.

One baby mutilated
so innocent and sweet.

One took his own life
as if the sun stopped
smiling.

One has to take
a life like making a
candle lose its flame.

One's gone mad like
Lucifer against God.

One's gone mad.
One's gone mad.

Leaders gone mad with power and greed.
The world's gone mad with war and suffering.
Life has gone mad with the endless torture of life and death.
The universe has gone mad within the endless void.
God's gone mad with power and destruction.
Everybody has gone mad, there is no escape from this torture, only suffering, only madness.

One's gone mad.

Varan Prem Anand (13)
Claires Court School, Maidenhead

Within My Blood

I gasp, cry out, stumble;
As blood, crimson, aglitter, menacing
Streams...
Down my trembling leg, coalescing
Tears, bite and gnaw into my cheeks like a piranha, stinging

Whilst my bursting ears are ringing...

I tussle and stumble through these incandescent, encaging, moonlit trees
However, within my pooling blood is
Heightening hope that I will
Abide, subsist,
Live...

Hairs on my stiff neck are standing tall like blades
Ready to melee.

Within my disconsolate blood, is escalating dismay.

Leaves are crunch, crunch, crunching beneath
My hollering feet.
Contorted roots are hurdles, whilst I flee.

Will I hold out, and continue to draw breath?
Or will I be in angst, right until my mutilating
Death?

George Lomas (13)
Claires Court School, Maidenhead

My Living Hell!

I awake to a startling scream!
I awake to spiders crawling on my walls!
My heart is thumping, racing, screaming for help -
My night has just begun

Fires rage as the earth crumbles at my feet
People screaming, whining to get help
Planets explode in the distance!
Monsters rise: mutated into my worst nightmare;

Spiders!

Their eight legs crawl up to my heart
Razor-sharp blades line the legs...

Suddenly...
I'm left there,
Trembling...

Crouched on the floor
Clutching my bleeding...
Heart!

I cry, wailing, begging to survive!
But it all goes dark? Why?

I awake again, hoping it's all a bad dream -
But it's happening again!
This is my living hell!

Vihaan Tailor (13)
Claires Court School, Maidenhead

The Earth

The Earth
The beautiful place
We all had in grace
The perfect place
But is it all safe?

Earth's colour is dying
Trees are lying
Dead on the floor
Awaiting for the roar
Of the man with the chainsaw...

The water was so clean
Why are people so mean?
The polluted water
The fish have been slaughtered
By the plastic floating above their head
Will be the reason they're dead

We don't deserve this world
We take it for granted
Deforestation, "But that doesn't matter."
We take it for greed
But soon we'll plead
For what we used to have

There's no more world peace
Earth's crumbling beneath our feet
Just for all of this, to repeat.

Toby Price (13)
Claires Court School, Maidenhead

Behind You

The harvest moon filled the sky,
My hopes and dreams whistled by.
As here it comes, we're face to face,
In his hand, his ruthless mace.

But something's wrong, something's off,
His hands were stuck, his hands were locked.
This wasn't him, this wasn't them,
He walked towards me once again.

He stopped in place, stared at my chest,
His big black jeans, his big black vest.
He looked at me, or so I thought,
I looked at what the mirror caught.

A man behind me, for all that time,
And my fate waits, in hands not mine.
I should've known, I should've seen,
The most feared man, right behind me.

Ollie Williamson (13)
Claires Court School, Maidenhead

The Alleyway

This. Is no normal alleyway.
This. Has a different feeling.
Something. I can't explain.

No one knows if it's legal. Or not.
You can always hear the explosions from science.
The Year 11s overcrowding our ears.
The overgrown bushes and spiderwebs.

The cracks and stones scattered around the patios.
The sides of mud. Dry and still.

The scariest turn. Always a heart-beater.
The doors wide open. Temptation.
My mind is flat.
What's in the door?
What are the low-level chats?

It's all making more sense.
The green electric fence.
The fence between school
And freedom.

Louis Manley (12)
Claires Court School, Maidenhead

In A Blink Of An Eye

In a blink of an eye, everything changed!
Running around, having fun with friends,
Then in a second, everything changed...
I got the worst injury
It changed my life
In a blink of an eye
I felt mad, I don't know why.
I fell into a dark place.
Didn't know if I could get out
I was sitting in my room, sad.
My friends who saw it happen came in
They helped me get fitter, better, happier and stronger
My injury eventually went away,
I thought to myself for a second
I said to myself, with the right people
I made it out of the dark place.
In a blink of an eye.

Harry Notton-Brown (12)
Claires Court School, Maidenhead

Can I Do It?

Can I do it? Can I?
I think I might give up.
This is impossible.
Why can't I write a stupid poem? (Sigh)
I think if I try a bit harder, I will be able to write this poem.
Nope. Didn't work.
This is so annoying!
Wait, I think I'm doing it. Yes. Don't give up now!
It is working.
So I can do it!
I am the best poet ever. I can do it.
No one can stop me now.
Wait, I think I just ran out of ideas.
This is pointless.
Why am I doing this anyway?
I remember why I am doing it -
To win the prize that I can easily win.
I can do it!

William Gowers (11)
Claires Court School, Maidenhead

The Beautiful Truth

Rain, thunder crashing down
Onto me, I just saw a clown,
Shivering now, I'm too scared,
I'm not rattled 'cause I cared,

The clown's back. Looking into me,
Is it all a dream? Or is it just me?

I hear scratching along my door,
Paint ripping down along, is it a poor
Helpless soul coming to deliver?
I now shiver.

I get scared at night,
When I'm home alone,
When the world is quiet,
And the demons do roam.
When the ghosts that haunt,
Invade my dreams,
I get scared at night.

Ethan Nation (14)
Claires Court School, Maidenhead

My Life...

The feeling I get from creating my own dishes
Is electrical
The enjoyment I get from it

Along with the planning for all the different parts
And segments for the dish

Heading to bookers, again out of burgers
Again out of buns
Again out of lemonade syrup
Again out of chips, again

Being shouted at by customers
Feet hurting
Spilling cooking oil again

Through all the negativity
I still love...

Fred Luke (13)
Claires Court School, Maidenhead

My RC Addiction

RC planes can go fast and in the wrong hands, they could go boom.

RC boats can go fast on water but on land, it's more of a stopper.

RC cars can do flips and tricks and you can get some high speeds, up to 35 to 40.

But my favourite has to be an RC car.

Because you can take them to skate parks and do cool stunts.

My RC addiction was from two people called Kevin Talbot and my dad.

So I have to say my biggest thank you to my dad and Kevin for helping me along the way.

Oscar Brown (11)
Claires Court School, Maidenhead

My Football Life

I wake up in the morning,
I hear the birds chirping.
I get my things.
I run to the car, very excited.
I can imagine us winning.
It's going to be fun.

I've got to the pitch.
The win will be done.
We start the match and I am a striker.
I have struck the goal and it was a screamer.
I celebrate with pride.
The sway of the trees, the lovely breeze
Makes the match much better.

I love football, it is my life.
I don't have a wife.
The match is done.
It was fun.

Robert O'Hagan (12)
Claires Court School, Maidenhead

Stormy Emotions

My anger was boiling deep down inside,
I couldn't hold it for any more time, I was smoking
Like a train with steam in the air,
Then everyone lost sight, then a terrified voice said,
"No, I want this to stop..."

All these strange changing emotions, this has to stop,
The anger all stopped and I dropped to the floor,
Thinking about my life to the core,
With all the pain now fell out from my core.

When you're in distress,
Stop, take a moment and take a rest.

Ewan Densley (11)
Claires Court School, Maidenhead

It Doesn't Matter Who You Are!

What if you couldn't hear?
What if there were many dangers without hearing?
But sometimes, it can be fun.
You can concentrate without sound.
But sometimes, it can be annoying.
You can't hear someone when they're talking,
You can't hear cars when they're coming.
But it doesn't matter.
Because I think
Having a disability is exceptional.
But all you need to remember from this poem,
Is that no matter who you are,
You are unique.

Rory Macmillan (11)
Claires Court School, Maidenhead

A Bad Feeling

Seeking eyes pierce my soul;
a lie becomes the truth untold,
an eerie presence beneath my feet;
quiet murmurs from across the street...

A whisper old, the story new;
a tale told, only by you.
A familiar face passing by;
chilling winds, high in the sky.

Strolling along a broken street;
a head held low, amidst defeat;
a shattered mystery, far from complete,
mistakes made, you cannot repeat.

Ah, the bittersweet taste of fear...

Sebastian Bose (13)
Claires Court School, Maidenhead

Eradicated

Eradicated
Assassinated
Decapitated
A flood of blood
I peek in the shadow
Chop the steak out of you
You can't bear this nightmare
You try to escape into a dream
But I shoot a beam
Through your chin
Put the blood in the bin
Cover up the evidence
Don't cry
You're just going to die
Run!
You don't know what I can become
You're going to die and bye

The end...
Of you.

Aarav Singh (12)
Claires Court School, Maidenhead

About Me

My favourite pizza is a margherita
Not a huge fan of a fajita

Playing with my friends is really fun
Riding on my bike in the bright, warm sun

I love gaming
And playing football when it's raining

I own many footballs
And enjoy eating Mum's meatballs

I enjoy exploring new places
And meeting new faces

With my family, I like chilling
Talking with them is interesting.

Jack Morrissey (12)
Claires Court School, Maidenhead

My Name

My name is Jake and I am not very tall,
I don't think I'm going to win this, not at all.
But my confidence keeps me going
And my memories keep me flowing.
I may not have done as well as the rest,
But I think I tried my best.
While writing this poem, while I'm going along,
I remain calm and remain strong.
Giving up is an option I'll never take.
Thank you for reading this, my name is Jake.

Jake Milborrow (11)
Claires Court School, Maidenhead

My Passion Is Rugby

I love the scrums,
pushing as hard as you can to get possession.
I cleared the ruck and passed it out to the winger;
we screamed as he dived to score the try.
We were 30-30; we needed to score.
We had a scrum.
I hooked the ball and Finlay passed it out
and ran as fast as he could to score the final try.
We cheered with happiness and joy.
We won, lads, come on 30-37,
three cheers for Marlow.

Dylan Moore (12)
Claires Court School, Maidenhead

Zombies

A once happy world,
Full of life.
Until everything unfurled.

Disease spread,
Everything mutated.
And if it wasn't,
It was dead!

At first, one came,
Then it was two.
Governments to blame,
They let them take over.

There's no going back,
Our world is now black.
Blood-curdling screams
Now fill our every dream!

Freddie Carpenter (13)
Claires Court School, Maidenhead

The Football Passion

We were 5-3 down, and it was getting desperate!
We were searching for the last two goals.

Like nothing else.

We got one goal, and now it was the final minute.
I put a cross in and it got kicked out.

Our defender took a touch.

Struck the ball and it rocketed
Into the top bins.

Absolute limbs!

Finlay Milner (13)
Claires Court School, Maidenhead

Gaming

Gaming is fun even when I run,
I like to play games every single day,
So this is why I play,
Even if I run, it's really, really fun.
Whenever I die, I really want to cry,
Sometimes I bail when I fail,
When I'm in a pickle, my mind sounds like a whistle,
Every new game I play,
Just feels like another day.

Thomas Kohler (12)
Claires Court School, Maidenhead

What I Want To Be

When I am older, I would like to play video games for money.
A bit funny, everybody wants money.
Even the bunny,
Who really just wants to fill his tummy.
Oh Mummy, could I have some money,
Just to buy something funny?
I'm such a dummy, I've lost all my money.

Barnaby Morgan (12)
Claires Court School, Maidenhead

Beaches

Well, all of a sudden, this has come to me -
the hate on beaches, something that doesn't appeal to me.
We show them hate, don't deny it, you know we do.
Litter on the sand, why can't we just adore it?
You run away from it, I'll come after you,
pick up that rubbish or you'll need a tissue.
Don't be childish, that's just wildish,
pick up your rubbish or you'll just be selfish.
I want to settle but I just can't,
every time I see a plastic bottle, I just crash.
An empty bag can affect our ocean.
Just, please, pick it up
and we'll have no negotiation.
Pollution. Pollution. Pollution -
Why do we have it?
We need to make it banished,
so let's make a start here.

Glenn McKerracher (13)
Clydeview Academy, Gourock

My First Gig

On the train on a Thursday afternoon,
nerves and excitement fill the room.
I step off the train, guitar in hand
and say to myself - I've done it! I'm in a band!
We're walking round Glasgow looking for eats,
if I don't get food, this day's incomplete.
We sit down in McDonald's while having something to eat,
the nerves now building even after this treat.
We walk down the road to Classic Grand
and buzz the door, saying, "We're the band!"
We walk up the stairs, thoughts filling our heads.
Are we great, are we awful?
If we're horrible,
this band's dead.
We walk through the door, gaze into the bar,
the stage, and say, "Soon, I'll be up there with my guitar."
Soon enough, the first band start, the people settle in.
In 30 minutes, they finish their set,
coming off the stage dripping in sweat.
After two more bands, on we get,
everything ready, still trying to be strong.
We're now on stage, the crowds have come in.
Then our leader singer shouts, "We're about to begin!"
I strum the first chord; the crowd scream and shout,
Is this the rock 'n' roll lifestyle all these bands sing about?

We play our last song, they want one more -
we all look at each other and say and think
Let's not bore!
So, we play one more song and walk off stage,
still everyone's shouting, as the next band starts to play.
So, that fear that I had has turned to excitement and happiness -
I don't care anymore, I will do it all again so happily.

Ruaridh McClure (13)
Clydeview Academy, Gourock

The Plastic Jellyfish

The sad plastic jellyfish of the sea,
The lifeless white is the first thing you'll see.
Oceans filled with this recyclable creature,
Even though it is never to be in nature.

In ten years time, you'll still be there,
Just bobbing around with one singular tear.
A fish gave you that, with just one bite,
A few hours later, the fish got a fright.

Wasting away like a flower with no sun,
Poisoning waters, yeah, that's what you've done.
It's weird to think that you were up there,
That you were used for carrying shopping for what people would wear.

You can be used for holding food,
But for the ocean, you are not good.
Holding stuff everywhere for everyone,
Even the people that are on the run!

Anyway, time to get to business -
If you see someone do this, you're my witness,
For everyone else, you're just a bag,
But if I see you swim, I gag.

I hope that we'll all agree
We should stop pollution, on three.

If we stop this now, our world will glisten,
And now I'd like to say, thanks for listening.

Katie Dunnet
Clydeview Academy, Gourock

Oh, How I Hate English!

Hundreds of books pinned up against the wall,
As I walk in with a smile on my face.
A good time in this room, I can't recall.
In this room, my mind becomes a disgrace.

I would rather be at home, all alone,
Than sit here and read, or write an essay.
It's almost as bad as breaking a bone.
I'd love to see this class in disarray.

The pale white jotters covered in writing.
Hundreds of piles of paper all lined up.
In here, watching the clock is nail-biting.
It's like drinking from a sharp, thorny cup.

When will this dreaded period finish?
All of this to say - oh, how I hate English!

Finley Buchan
Clydeview Academy, Gourock

Wonderful KFC

When you walk up to the big KFC,
Oh, the wonderful things you'll see!
The whiff of tasty fried chicken
Might just make you feel awe-stricken.

With the big KFC logo staring into your soul,
Turning you into a chicken black hole!
The salt on your lips as you eat the chips
Like a sponge soaking up the crispiness.

Go in and see, all them eating
And your heart starts beating.
Then you eat the fillets with their tender taste,
Love the smell of grease and the diamond shape.

But then, the restaurant is closing,
So you grab everything before they start disposing!

Xander Young (13)
Clydeview Academy, Gourock

Art

In this world, art is simple.
The art there was, is no longer here.
If it were brought back, would it be more able?
It used to be here, but now it's over there.
Over there, it's a clue!
But now it's just so. Blue.
But that isn't here, I'm sure there's a tear.
Old art is crumbling, modern art is rising,
So little work, so major in price.
Old art is fading, modern art is roaring,
So major in work, so little in price.
So simple yet so loved,
So hard yet so despised.
There's a house over there,
But that doesn't mean there's life.

Amy MacLellan
Clydeview Academy, Gourock

Vapes

This cloud of smoke gasses the town,
Destroying people's run-down lives,
Drowning, as people want it gone.
Shouting loudly for it to go.

These ghastly things haunting the town.
The sunlight vanishing into thin air.
They tried their best, but it isn't enough.
The quest continues further.

Given up smoking, but this isn't much better.
Spiralling out of control like super-fast wheels,
An outbreak like the Black Death,
People dying from this cancerous breath.

Horrid vapes, we want you gone,
Horrid vapes, we want you gone!

Flynn McLellan (13)
Clydeview Academy, Gourock

The Effect Of Music

Lively cheering from every direction,
My brain flooded with energetic emotion.
They stand bold on that stage, no fear to see.
They play their sick tunes, everyone's keen
For them to keep going but stop, they soon must.
However, live in the moment, in music we trust.

It helps me get away from my issues.
When my feelings have been battered and abused,
I stick in my AirPods to stop the insanity,
A nice and easy way to escape from reality.

So next time you feel dejected, downcast or depressed,
Shove some noise on your headphones, and drown out the rest.

Mikey Cardona
Clydeview Academy, Gourock

Dream

The skyscrapers towering over me,
So tall in the sky but so close to me.
The crowds, they come like wind,
Blowing them in on the weekends.
Food trucks and the big long lines that gather.
The smell of cooking, it doesn't matter.
It's the way I want my life,
Just wait for the nightlife.
The chaos like animals scrambling in the wild,
The dream has always been in my mind.
One day, I'll be in that part.
One day, I'll get what I want.
One day, you won't disapprove.
One day, I will move.

Katie Sullivan (13)
Clydeview Academy, Gourock

Shoes

Your house? Your car? Your fancy China bowl?
What would you give for a pair of shoes
Without selling your soul?
Shoes the same price as a cruise,
You really have nothing to lose!
Walking for a mile in style,
I can hear the blisters whisper through the thick leather.
Jimmy Choos are barely even shoes,
Louboutin heels are like walking on wheels.
Whatever the occasion,
Whatever the outfit,
Find comfort and style in every shoe.

Ellie Stewart (13)
Clydeview Academy, Gourock

Truth

I have not won Truth's favour,
For her bitter hands blind me.
She has not allowed me to share her grace.
She hides the very essence of her beauty from me.
The forgiveness, life, acceptance and relief,
Laced together to form her tender soul.
Yet that is for her favourable.

For us, we are left with the numbing chills,
The strangling grasp of her hands,
And only our pitiful tears to warm us.
We are left drowning in inexplicable sorrow,
And our desires for what could have been.
The alternate future where she did not claw her way in.
That other life, the ember of love or illusions we wished to live.

Yet she grins as she steals and reduces them to cinders.
For she is the burden Man must endure for eternity.
She constantly forges destruction,
Leaving us to tread on the sharpened fragments of her existence.

We who are unfavoured by Truth,
'Unlucky' and 'unfavourable' are we.
For we trudge through the residue she leaves,
With the hands of ignorance blinding us.

Ruqaya El (15)
Hereford Cathedral School, Hereford

Truth, Beautiful?

Beauty is truth, truth beauty, -that is all
Ye know on earth, and all ye need to know

That's what Keats tries to show

But when my makeup's smeared, I'm told to correct it
When I'm bawling my eyes out, I'm told to fix it
When I'm broken on the floor
Then I'm considered a bore

I'm just done
Oh, how I wish I could run

I would run to the hills, far away
Oh, and how I would start to pray
Praying for someone to save me
Please, I plea
You have to get me out of here.
Can anyone hear?

Instead, I must splash my face
And walk confidently out into the space
And hide my scars, wear my mask
And pray people don't ask

When I'm stood in a bar
That's when I'm called a star
When I'm in my short dress
That is when they say yes

But that is not my truth.

What is my truth?
That's the question they never ask

My truth is that I'm broken from the past
I do not know how long I'll last
How much longer the past can hold me
My heart wishes it could flee
To flee to the mountains from the ghosts that haunt me

But no one can see.
My truth is invisible.
The wind's sorrow unconditional

Can anyone hear?
I'm drowning, please save me

And yet you tell me the truth is beautiful?

Anna Price (16)
Hereford Cathedral School, Hereford

Let The Ships Sink

You are not defined by the colour of your hair,
How much you know
Or what you wear.

You are not defined by the way you speak,
The way you stutter
Or if you even decide to peep.

You are *not* defined by how much you *weigh*,
How much you eat
Or what the scales display.

I wish I spoke in the way that I think,
If it's the truth I let out
Then why not let ships sink?

You are defined by your beautiful laugh,
Your greying hairs
Not whether you fit on a graph.

If I spoke in the way that I think:
Aggressively, obsessively, un-repressively,
I would talk my way to the point of suffocation,
I would preach to the point of no self-preservation.
But everyone would know exactly how I felt,
About the way they degrade themselves.

"I hate my hair and what I wear,
The way I stutter, the way I mutter,

I hate my weight, and how much I ate."
Voice the bravest people of late.

I wish I spoke with the hunger in which I think:
Ambitiously, passionately, ferociously.
Then the masses would know.

You are not defined by how you look,
Your height, your strife,
Or whether you can read a book.

I am now writing in the way that I think:
Ambitiously, aggressively, slightly egotistically,
It's time to let the ships sink.

Astrid Westerlund (14)
Hereford Cathedral School, Hereford

The Beautiful Truth

T o begin this poem, I'd like to say that I truly do
H ate you. And one day, I should like to wave goodbye
E ven though my heart shall turn bitter and blue

B ut hearts can be shocked back to beating
E nergy waves electrifying capillaries and veins
A ll my faint memories of you deleting
U ntil one day, I see your face in a tainted mirror
T hose faint memories of you flooding back
I 'll scream and smash my image like a killer
F ighting away the tears - my baby hands gory
U ntil I no longer recognise myself, grisly and cold
L ike a witch in some happy children's story

T rust me when I say this, hold my baby hand, I will
R un away like a comet flying across a night sky
U nified in my independence, living for simply the thrill
T hank you for sneaking and stealing my youth, I
H ate you, and that, my friends, is the beautiful truth.

Sylvie Hart (16)
Hereford Cathedral School, Hereford

Be Beautiful, Be True!

Scrolling, I see people prettier than me
Their flawless skin, how are they so thin?
My soul starts to hollow from the people that I follow
How can I be more like them and not like me?

If I tweak my photo here and edit my features there
Maybe more people will like it and finally, they will care
Likes will give me a friend, no one will know it's pretend
But will I ever feel free if I'm not truly being me?

I start to realise, it's not just me in disguise
Every page is the same, how does this bring fame?
How do people really look behind their TikTok and Facebook?
Surely this isn't cool, why was I such a fool?

If I don't want to feel alone, I must put down the phone
I want people to see the true version of me
Everyone is unique and that's what we should seek
So don't follow the crowd, stand up and be proud
Be beautiful, be true, I'll be me and you be you...

Milly Clarke (11)
Hereford Cathedral School, Hereford

The Warmth That Was

It came as the first summer's dawn,
It beamed on us as does the sun,
We lived within its bound as though they'd never end,
But fleeting in the summer, and dawn fades into dusk.

When love beckons, you do follow,
But as for it - 'tis a burning thing,
Unyielding fire, providing either comfort or suffering.

And as the summer left,
The sun set. What was warmth,
Became coldness.
Within us, the winter dwelt,
Separating our hearts,
Freezing our joy into pain and,
Our smiles into frowns.

But 'til next summer,
When the sun will beam on us once more,
Melting us back our smiles.

If only the summer lasted,
The things I'd give for the sun's return,
For it to reignite our love.

It came as the first summer's dawn,
And left us on the dewy winter's morn,

But 'tis gone with the harsh gales of time,
And shan't return yet, for a while.

Kyro Hanna (16)
Hereford Cathedral School, Hereford

Cracks

When I was 12, I sat down and travelled through my mind.
Looked at everything, all the dust and cracks,
Whilst I sat with my back against a towering oak,
I cried.

For at the end, I had found a door,
With rainbow haze creeping out of the cracks.
I ran away from it, and tried to forget,
As I knew what the repercussions would be of opening it.

When I was 14, I went back,
And turned open the lock on that door,
Slowly.
So very slowly.

And I peered through the crack of the open door.

And to my surprise, I found
Everything I had hoped for and more.
My hopes and dreams, my wishes and secrets,
But the thing I dreaded most stood right in front of me.

It reached out to me, and I saw myself reaching
Towards the thing that I thought would destroy me.
But instead, I found much more,
I had found a home that I had ignored.

I had found me.

Ellen Carroll (15)
Hereford Cathedral School, Hereford

My Silence Is My Self-Defence

My silence is my self-defence
What would I be if I shed this guise?
What secrets could be seen deep in my eyes?
Magnified by tears that nurture my disdain,
My soul laid bare, exposed to the pain.

My smile, a shelter from what's out of reach,
Afraid of the truths that I dare not teach.
My greatest fear is that you see me,
The way I see myself to be.

If the mask should fall, would you stay near?
Or turn away, consumed by fear?
For shadows I hide might darken your view,
And change the way you see me too.

But perhaps, in the light of my soul's release,
I'd find in the truth a kind of peace.
Though fragile, I stand with all I conceal,
Longing to know if I'm worthy and real.

The words unspoken weigh heavy inside,
A fortress of fear where I choose to hide.
I bury my thoughts at truth's expense,
For my silence is my self-defence.

Theo Gerrand (15)
Hereford Cathedral School, Hereford

You Don't Know Me

You don't know me,
What I hide behind my smile,
All the pain I burrow away,
You don't know what I have been through,
You don't know what I am currently going through,
You don't know where I am from,
You don't know my background,
You don't know my family,
You don't know what I have seen.
Yet, I still greet everyone I see
I still say thank you to a cashier,
I still move out of the way for people on the streets,
I still help people,
I still respect everyone and everything.
Can't you?
You don't know the real world,
Take it for granted,
You haven't seen your whole family drop to the floor dead,
You haven't seen the horrible scenes of war,
You haven't seen your whole world crumble beneath your feet,
You haven't seen a child who has lost everything it knows,
You haven't seen what life can be like in the real world,
Do you ever just stop and think?
So, do you really know me?

Sian Howells (12)
Hereford Cathedral School, Hereford

Lost Between Worlds

I see the world behind the screen,
It moves, it grows as rivers flow.
Yet I am here, a ghost of mind,
Sat here still as I leave it all behind.

The days slip past in pixel light,
I swipe through life, but never fight -
Each flicker of the glowing screen
Pulls me deeper, caught between.

Dreams are chased, laughter spread -
Friends fall in love, stars shift overhead.
The Earth has spun, the children grown,
But I am still, this screen my home.

I watch it all, the seasons blend,
And wonder when my time will end,
I feel the guilt beneath my skin,
"I should be more!" But I hide within.

The world calls out, I stay away,
Afraid to leave, afraid to stay.
The world outside is rushing fast,
Each year dissolves like smoke, like glass,
But I am stuck in an endless scroll,
A silent figure with a lost soul.

Naiya Davidson (15)
Hereford Cathedral School, Hereford

Love Yourself, Be Who You Are

The world is such a lively, beautiful place
Full of dreams, ambitions and goals to chase
Packed with new sights, tastes, emotions and more
Influencers, social media and people you adore
Distractions of your phone, shopping feeds greed
Making you want things you don't need
Anger, frustration, it's easy to feel
Sometimes, there are moments that don't seem real
Little sleep and a tired mind
A place of peace is what you must find
Don't give up and be your best
And make sure you're healthy and get lots of rest
Love yourself, yourself, you're a star
You being you makes you who you are
And this is a reminder to embrace your life
If you hold back from joy, you'll only feel less alive
The world is big and the universe is wide
But it doesn't matter how big the challenge is
It's about what's inside.

Annabelle Jackson (12)
Hereford Cathedral School, Hereford

The Ocean Blue

When the waves crash and the wind is high
The ship sets sail as the night goes by.

Why, oh why do they roam at night?
The wind will give them quite a fright
The waves will send them back to bay
Mother Nature will have her way.

When the waves crash and the wind is high
The ship sets sail as the night goes by.

Big Mother Blue goes round and round
Trying to keep her calf around
All night long and through the day
The threats all slowly go away.

When the waves crash and the wind is high
The ship sets sail as the night goes by.

Turtles at the surface and anchovies below
And on the water above rests the evening glow
Anglers at the bottom, being the highlight
Others just prefer being in the twilight.

When the waves crash and the wind is high
The ship sets sail as the night goes by.

Matilda Driver (11)
Hereford Cathedral School, Hereford

Be Yourself?

Be yourself, they say.
They make it sound easy.
Like you should know, at this moment,
Who you are.

How do you know who you are -
Find yourself when stuck in a box?
When they keep you
From discovering what the world has to offer?

How should I know who I am
When the ones instructing me
To have it all figured out
Hide me from opportunity?

Let me leave
And get lost in the world.
Maybe in doing so
I will find myself.

Because you don't need to know
Who you are
Or why you're here
At the age of fifteen.

You don't need to know
Who you want to be when you grow up
At forty-nine or eighty-one.
Because solving the puzzle of your own mind takes time.

So, give us all that time.
Let us learn who we are
Before you ask us
To be ourselves.

Laura Dean (15)
Hereford Cathedral School, Hereford

I'm Human

I'm human
I'm not perfect
I make mistakes
I say the wrong things
And sometimes do the wrong things
But it's all right because I'm human

I'm not the prettiest
I'm not the smartest
I'm not the funniest
Not the fastest nor the kindest
But it's all right because I'm human

Sometimes I get tired,
Tired of the friends I have acquired
Tired of school
Tired of waking up each day just to sit on a stool
But it's all right because I'm human

So when I see someone smile
Because of something I did
Or improve on a test that last time was quite mid
And I wake up and smile because I just love living
That's the best bit of just being a human being

You can enjoy the small things in life
And my life may not be a perfect sight
But that's all right.

Martha Trafford-Roberts
Hereford Cathedral School, Hereford

Climate Change

Once upon a time,
When dinosaurs ruled the land,
Planet Earth was flourishing,
And everything was hand in hand,

But now take a look around,
And see what the world has become,
A deteriorating planet
What have us humans done?

Our land is heating up,
Deforestation is happening,
The animals have fewer homes,
Carbon dioxide is increasing,

Litter is dropped on the floor,
And finding its way into the seas,
Marine animals are dying from it
At the worst rate we've seen,

Over in Antarctica,
The icebergs are melting
The polar bears have no place to go,
And the humans really aren't helping,

So if we all work together,
And clean up this planet,

Our world will be saved
And it will be like there was never any damage.

Rowan McIntyre (11)
Hereford Cathedral School, Hereford

The Wonders Of The World

We have shaped our beautiful planet,
But we have forgotten how to plan it,
For our children's future.
We have chosen to fish the seas,
To kill off animals,
Cut down trees,
But forgotten to think,
Even for a moment,
That do we really, truly own it?
Shop-bought stuff,
It is a sin,
That everything we eat has plastic in.
In our fish,
In our greens,
So can everyone just stop,
Please,
And think,
For a moment.
Have we taken it too far?
Have we gone above the bar?
Population is rising fast,
And who knows how long it will last
Before it stops,
And we're left adrift in empty space.
Like bits of dust,
Out of place.

But if we change,
And we stop,
And we start afresh,
Who knows what wonders will wait there for us?

Gelliert Thacker-Vuts (13)
Hereford Cathedral School, Hereford

Drifting Away

Whilst scrolling on our screens,
we lose the day,
hours slip silently,
drifting away.

Eyes fixed on pixels,
time stands still,
yet the world outside
still moves at its will.

Minutes turn to hours,
unnoticed and unseen,
in the digital realm,
where we've always been.

The clock ticks on,
but we don't hear,
lost in our screens,
time disappears.

Moments pass
as we carry on in the night,
we miss the dawn
and the morning light.

Screens hold our gaze,
our minds confined,
while the hands of time,
we cannot find.

We need to break free,
lift our eyes,
see the world
beneath the skies.

For time is precious,
fading fast,
so cherish each moment
and make it last.

Grace Clokie (13)
Hereford Cathedral School, Hereford

Nostalgia

I look through my photos every day,
Through times full of joy and times of dismay.
I see times of love and times of sorrow,
And wonder what I will see tomorrow.

I look through my photos from last year,
Such happy times, yet my eyes fill with tears.
Seeing the person I was, full of stress,
I realise everything has changed, even how I dress.

I look through my photos from childhood days,
And I think of how those years were so different from today's.
In photos with old friends, I'm wild and free,
Looking happily at the world, faces full of glee.

But then I look through my photos from this week,
And I realise how much I've grown, no longer timid or meek.
I see myself, full of happiness, love, curiosity,
And I realise there is no one else I'd rather be.

Honor Watts (15)
Hereford Cathedral School, Hereford

The Museum

I went to the museum but what I saw will amaze,
A twenty-foot ape with a big scary gaze,
A lion with courage that never will shed,
A horse's heart that's bigger than my head,
But the last thing was in a cage dark and red,
I pressed my face close, couldn't believe my eyes,
A hognose snake swallowing a rat in disguise,
But what happened next will make you feel dizzy,
The massive snake was busy,
Wriggling out of its dark cage, a massive ape,
A twenty-foot beast with a mighty escape,
And all the animals, wild in their strife,
In the museum came surging to life
Partying and partying till morning was nigh,
They climbed the building till they were high,
With a view of the city,
The sunrise rose,
And then they stood still until the museum had closed.

Finlay Webb (11)
Hereford Cathedral School, Hereford

Consistency

The work begins without a sound,
No honour here, no cheering crowd.
I doubt the mission, I doubt the way,
Yet still, I stand and face the day.

Each motion feels like moving sand,
The weight of doubt within my hand.
But something shifts in silence deep -
A change unfolds where shadows sleep.

I yearn for proof, for signs of worth,
But effort alone can feel like curse.
The mirrors deceive; no dawn in sight,
And yet I work through the night.

Until one day, I feel the shift -
A flame once cold begins to lift.
For in the dark, through endless grind,
The self I sought, I slowly find.

So let it be, the lesson clear:
In every trial, a truth unfolds.
With sweat and grit, the heart draws near,
What you invest is what you hold.

Leonidas Morphis (15)
Hereford Cathedral School, Hereford

An Eye For An Eye

I skip down the road, darker and darker it grows,
The decoration tombstone,
The skeletons, the wrappers, the bones,
Something glares, an eye for an eye?

Trick or treat? It echoes in my head,
Prank ideas come and go,
Surely there's something that's better instead,
Something stares, an eye for an eye?

Something behind? No surely not,
Girls skip by,
A witch's cauldron a crackling pot,
An idea shared, an eye for an eye?

Windows are shut, it makes me scared,
Babies bawl never good,
Now's for the teens and they don't care,
My mind dared, an eye for an eye?

It leaps out on me, one great screech,
I jump from my skin, one great eek,
He sticks to me, like a leech,
Only my brother. An eye for an eye!

Luke Williamson (11)
Hereford Cathedral School, Hereford

Imagine

Imagine a world as you close your eyes,
as darkness falls, as the barn owl flies
Moths flutter, bats squeak, circling through the air,
whilst you leap off into your dreams,
even though you're not there
Accelerating upwards though you have no speed,
breaking out of the clouds, being freed
Gliding, soaring to a dazzling height,
watching the eagle displaying his might
Igniting the sky with millions of birds,
a murmuration of starlings, focused then blurred
Northern Lights flicker, passing through my head
as I tumble gently back into my bed
Effervescent rays blind me as I open my eyes,
the chattering dawn chorus welcomes me as I rise.

Romilly Elliott (11)
Hereford Cathedral School, Hereford

Letting Go

I watched the autumn leaves descend,
Their journey light, without a bend.
No struggle in the wind's embrace,
Just quiet trust in time and space.

The branches know when to release,
To shed the weight and find their peace.
For in the fall, new life is born,
And only empty hands can mourn.

I gather moments like scattered sand,
Clutching tightly what slips from my hand.
Yet with each grain that fades from sight,
I find the strength to seek the light.

I witnessed the rivers softly flow,
From oceans to other oceans below.
Through forests and towns without strife,
Embracing change throughout their life.

The echoes of what once was near,
Turn into whispers, soft and clear.
In every loss, a lesson glows,
And through the dark, a new path grows.

Sophia O'Leary
Hereford Cathedral School, Hereford

Gratitude's Glow

I wanted this more,
Yet hate my gifts,
Longing for things,
In a world full of rifts.

Loneliness creeps,
A shadow at my side,
Why, oh why,
Do my dreams have to hide?

Family's embrace,
What I asked, not in sight,
Regrets fill my heart,
In the stillness of night.

Thoughts once so bright,
Now fade in the fray,
Instead of desire,
I'll cherish today.

Though wishes may linger,
And hopes often sway,
Gratitude blooms,
In its own gentle way.

Be happy with what,
In your life, you hold dear,
For love's quiet whispers
Are what truly endear.

So keep peace above,
Let kindness unfold,
And maybe one day,
Your dreams will be told.

Avitej Singh
Hereford Cathedral School, Hereford

Untitled

Dancing in the rain with the one I call my love
Our feet move to the music, from the big band in the sky;
The sun has since left us and is hidden high above
While the lampposts stand in awe as if wondering passers-by.

My dress appears different, and his suit and tie too
The addition of the raindrops make his kiss cherry-sweet;
The love we have between us will remain ever true
Although the time is only around until night turns to noon.

So, for now, just spin me around this dance floor,
Get me drunk on love like yours, we've got until the sun shows;
I know that tomorrow I'll be standing at the door
I think that maybe it is time for the curtains of this dance to close.

Ruth Mattos (16)
Hereford Cathedral School, Hereford

Trapped

I am trapped
Somebody has taken my breath away
Constricted, gasping
Not okay not that I can say
I am not able to run or jump
Not able to wear the clothes I want
Always afraid it will show through
A problem whenever I try something new

Even though I'm twisted on the inside
I don't want it to affect my life
Why with no pain
With nothing on show
Do I have to do this
Unable to say no

When the sun is beating down
In the heat, I slowly drown
This casing, this shell I can't shake off
Even when everyone else is cooling off
I am trapped
And I am stuck this way
Until I'm fully grown
Though when that is no one can say.

Alice Morris Dawson (13)
Hereford Cathedral School, Hereford

Untitled

If your passion is like a fire,
Blood running deep with desire,
Don't let it wither and die,
Don't listen to the perfect lie,
Your dream's too big, the goal too wide
Don't force it down, don't make it hide
Let your fire burn brighter and brighter
Keep pushing, keep going, keep being a fighter

Don't just sit down and quit
Come on, you can take those hits
Whatever your dream
An astronaut, or playing on a football team
Don't give in, pursue it till the end
Cause no matter how hard you hit, you can always mend
Victory is yours, yours for the taking
The world is yours, and nothing is beyond your making.

George Martin (15)
Hereford Cathedral School, Hereford

A Timeless World

D Ms sent, constantly ringing in the recipient's ear,
O blivious of the hours flying by as you scroll.
N ew friend requests pop up, ignoring those more dear,
T roubled by the image of self, becoming a mental health toll.

W ebsite to website, no real objective,
A ddiction? No, I can stop! I just don't want to...
S ocial anxiety brimming, spiralling out of perspective,
T oxic groups messaging all night, but it's fine, they are still your crew?
E nhanced photos, entranced teens, their meaning nuanced.

I nadvertent consumption of that most precious commodity:
T ime...

Huw Pritchard (16)
Hereford Cathedral School, Hereford

They Live Among Us

They spawn in the lobby, hearts are cold,
The crewmates working, secrets they hold,
Their tasks to finish, their lives at stake,
Among us, there is no room for mistake.

Red is sus, in the chat they say,
Innocent crewmates fear each passing day,
Sabotage and vents they sneak,
If they seem sus, their future looks bleak.

Emergency meetings, votes cast wide,
Who's the impostor? They can't decide,
Innocence swears, from the impostor they hide,
One by one, the innocent died.

Ejected into the silent void,
A crewmate's trust, now destroyed,
Victory in the balance, thin,
A game of wits, to lose or win.

Owain Howells (15)
Hereford Cathedral School, Hereford

The Power Of A Book

I sit down and open my book
Then place myself in my favourite nook
The fantasy world unfolds
And devours me within its magical world
I lose myself in caves and corals
And stand my ground against dragons and trolls
And people get cured from being cursed
While princes fight off evil, undeterred
Stories travel around the world
'Til they find their place with boys and girls
Life must go on, but I am stuck
Imagining fairy tale plots
I can't escape my own brain
Or the world, so very plain
So, reluctantly, I close my book and exit my nook
And return to the world where I feel misunderstood
And sadly, call my own.

Matilda Judd (14)
Hereford Cathedral School, Hereford

The Wonder Of Football

Excitement builds,
and we're all so thrilled,
but who will win
and wear the grin?
All of us waiting for the whistle
to see the most skilful,
swarming round the ball like angered bees,
socks pulled up past our knees.
Opponents score first,
the feelings are the worst,
heads down, we equalise,
we lift our arms to the skies,
don't settle for the draw,
let's keep pushing for more.
Never give up, be a dreamer,
thirty yards out and he scores a screamer,
dads all cheer,
but the mums shed a tear.
Relief and joy as we lift up the cup,
we all said to ourselves, "Never give up!"

Edward White (11)
Hereford Cathedral School, Hereford

What Is Left Of The Beautiful Truth

You and I
We are children of bones and flesh and blood
Yet below the skin, it claws at my guilt
Nagging, taunting, beckoning
A perpetual, irreparable scag in the fabric of my being
If only serpents were not so tempting
If only apples were not so delicious
My story is scribed
In an old felted tome
Bound with a needle and thread
And laced with regret and fear for the future
As the ink etches itself on the parchment
The ever-throbbing tide slowly
Cleanses me, but in turn
Scatters the fragments of what is left of the truth
The beautiful truth
Which is becoming harder and harder to grasp.

Daisy Fleetwood (14)
Hereford Cathedral School, Hereford

My Poem

In the twilight's gentle sway,
Where dreams and whispers come to play,
A world unfolds, calm and bright,
Under the stars, in the shaded night.
Soft winds dance with leaves very fine,
Whispers of an ancient time,
Where love and hope, like shadows blend,
And every journey will find its end.
In all our hearts, a story lies,
A tale of sorrow, joy, and bright skies,
Where every tear and every smile,
Makes our life's journey a well worthwhile.
So, as we walk, hand in hand,
Through this enchanted forest,
Remember this, my dear and true,
The greatest poems are me and you.

George Brown (11)
Hereford Cathedral School, Hereford

Prison Cell Phone

Stop. Pause. Look, there's a world you need to see
Don't miss the bird calling beneath the tree

Your phone is like a magnet pulling you in
So succeed and don't let it win

Deer look so happy frolicking past
Pay attention to the real world for joy that will last

Running through fields of daisies is an escape to reality, let the world feel
We need to lock down our phones, allowing us to heal

When we were young, our smiles were never fake
Our minds were full of Christmas and birthday cake

Be a kid, play outside
Live life, it's a wild ride.

Daisy Hall (13)
Hereford Cathedral School, Hereford

Sails And Trails Of The North

In the land where the fjords meet the sky,
Where the summits of the so-ever-high mountains lie,
Covered with their frost-coated peaks,
Through the blizzard, everything looks bleak.

The northern lights dance in colours so bright,
Greens, pinks and blues fill the heavens with light,
From Oslo's bright streets to Trysil's crests,
With eagles soaring back to their cosy nests.

So here in the land of the Viking's proud heart,
Where nature and culture are never apart,
Majestic animals nestle in the fern tree,
Norway, dear Norway, you are home to me.

Jacob Denslow (14)
Hereford Cathedral School, Hereford

Nature's True Peace

The breeze whips my face, dancing and smiling
Birdsong frolics, a beautiful melody of tweets and tunes
The sea bellows, azure and flying
I can just be myself when I am with nature

Each of the birds I spot as I wonder
Is different in colour, shape and song
They are all so precious, no matter the appearance
They are feathered gems with wings.

The colours all fly as I gaze out to the sea
I find peace in the things others cannot
Although I cannot fit into the puzzle others have made,
I am different, I am a nature-lover, unique and fully me.

Olive York Moore (12)
Hereford Cathedral School, Hereford

A World Without Phones

Phones
Spreading news
Even if it isn't true
Allowing people to send unkind texts
Showing children things they shouldn't see
Making people addicted and longing for devices
Children always on phones, never outside in nature
Making everyone angrier and more anti-social
But a world without phones would be full of fun
Children playing together outside in the fresh air
Reading reliable news from the papers
Writing letters to people with a pen
Playing games with family
Everyone happier
A world without
Phones.

Isla Storey (12)
Hereford Cathedral School, Hereford

Perfect

Autumn or fall,
A season for all.
The photos look golden,
With leaves tumbling down.
Red petals graze the floor,
Like a picture from folklore.
The perfect frame,
For the perfect person.
The perfect smile,
On the perfect face.
The truth, the key,
You don't want to be them.
They're not happy,
They worry about pictures and posts.
They're not flawless,
No one ever is.
Don't strive to be like them,
You'll never achieve.
Because perfect is something,
Not for you nor me.

Evie Prowse (11)
Hereford Cathedral School, Hereford

The Same

If not the same then what are you?
If you don't know look around
Because there's a chance no one has a clue
Shut your eyes and hear for a sound
In a sea full of green you are what turns blue
One in a million could be mimed
Or could we be a thousand found in time

Or could you be a grain of salt in a sea of sand
What was considered could not be found
As if we fight with only one hand
Thinking only one is down to the ground
But you could be found or drowned
The chance of death could not be bound.

Reuben Alcott (15)
Hereford Cathedral School, Hereford

Dreams

My parents won the lottery
We moved into town
My friends came over more often
I got everything I wanted.
Almost.
I grew up
I got a partner
I got a good job
I worked as a doctor.
A surgeon.
I had kids, they grew up
I got a message on my phone
They died in a car crash
Along with my partner.
I got fired.
I couldn't pay the house bills alone.
Then I heard a bell ring loudly
And here I am
Picking up my bag, making my way over to the next boring lesson
Was that all a lie?

Bethany Hodgson-Hutton (13)
Hereford Cathedral School, Hereford

The Beautiful World

Oh, beautiful world with the most sunny skies.
The lush green grass once as white as clouds.
Oh, beautiful world the beach yellow as the bright sun.
Hear the people play in the sunshine having so much fun running around.
Oh, beautiful world with lush oceans that have emotion.
What can the world offer more?
Oh, beautiful world with the lights in the night sky.
The world as curled as a ball in the sky
Oh, world with trees as green as the north light
The world with the most colourful wonders of the universal.

Jack Evans (11)
Hereford Cathedral School, Hereford

Life Online

In the glow of screens, our lives unfold,
One click away to another story told,
Connections made with a swipe or click,
In this online world, time moves quick.

Eyes damaged with blue light's stare,
Captured pixels in the air,
Scrolling through moments old and new,
Memories remembered by a few.

Cherish the moments both online and real,
So let us take time away from our phones to let our brain heal,
So let us remember, in this online space,
To seek the human, face to face.

Annie Wall (13)
Hereford Cathedral School, Hereford

Let The Real Me Show

I am the morning light
I am the dancer at night
I am the candle that glows
I am the seasons' show

Through ups and downs, I find the key
The truths of being me
I am the spark, I glow
In every moment, I learn to grow

I won't hide, I'll let it show
Let the real me glow
I won't hide, I'll shine so bright
In every struggle, I'll find what's right

In every moment, I'll let love send
The message of truth, where hearts can blend.

Lucy Olivia Forker (12)
Hereford Cathedral School, Hereford

Don't Hide Behind Your Smile!

Don't hide behind your smile
Like a child behind their mother
Be as open as a pack of crisps
To people

Don't tell people you're fine when you're not
Like on a rugby pitch
You should tell people that you feel bad on the inside
And not smile to cover it up

People who hide behind their smiles
Are only making things harder for themselves

What do you think friends are for?
They are there to help, so tell them anything
Or tell your parents.

Tom Norman (13)
Hereford Cathedral School, Hereford

Phones

I'm having a great time on my brand-new phone
I just can't put it down! And
So don't tell me
You would have so much more fun outside
Because I believe that
There's nothing wrong with scrolling through TikTok
There's no point you arguing that
Phones are pointless time wasters
You can't change my opinion -
Phones are great!
There's no way I will join you when you say
We can look at this another way

Now read from bottom to top.

Charlotte Middleton (13)
Hereford Cathedral School, Hereford

Climate Change

I believe the world needs to change
There is no other planet to do an exchange
World leaders need to speak the truth
About the damage of our world to the youth
The ice is melting, we must stop it
So much destruction to rainforests for profit
The signs of climate change everywhere
So sadly, animals and birds becoming more rare
Countries should be held to account
As all the problems continue to mount
Let us stop and take action today
Soon, the planet may not see another day.

Alice Blandford (13)
Hereford Cathedral School, Hereford

Hidden

In a world full of screens,
Voices echo but I can't stay,
Behind the filters, I hide my face,
In a crowded room, I find no space.

Scrolling through lives, a silent scream,
Chasing connections, lost in a dream,
Though I'm online, I feel so apart,
A hidden soul with a heavy heart.

Wishing for moments real and true,
Yet trapped in a feed, I can't break through,
Longing for laughter, a touch, a sign,
To step from the shadows and truly shine.

Maisie Fenner (14)
Hereford Cathedral School, Hereford

Shepherd Or Sheep?

From fashion vogue to the latest craze
We look for the spark in the digital maze
We scroll through feeds, lost in a daze

With every moment, we are part of the show
As we leave our mark in the new

As friends send others the latest trends
But don't stay for long before they are gone

Stories unfold as the new unravels
As all duplicate the original
Very few set the new

In everybody's journey, a shared embrace
We all have to face!

Fearn Middleton (13)
Hereford Cathedral School, Hereford

People Watching

I gaze through the glass, my life slipping away,
Hours, I spend watching people,
Some of whom I see every day, some of whom I'll never see again,
All I see is a few seconds of their day,
But from these moments, I make assumptions, false assumptions mainly,

Rarely do I stop and think, think about what their lives are really like.
We don't see the bad moments,
We don't see the silent battles faced,
Hours spent to select,
So we only see the perfect.

Issy North (15)
Hereford Cathedral School, Hereford

Fake Friends

In the glow of screens, they come and go,
With words so sweet, like a gentle flow,
Promises made in the virtual light,
But vanish quickly into the night.

They wear masks of kindness so bright,
Yet behind the pixels, they hide from sight,
Their friendship fades, was it all pretend?

In the world of likes and fame,
True connections can be hard to find,
So cherish those who stand by your side,
In the real world, hearts don't hide.

Stanley McIntyre (13)
Hereford Cathedral School, Hereford

Night Beauty

The night is clear, crisp, calm
Your luminescence stops me
The natural beauty
Spellbound
I am drawn to your splendour
The frost under my feet
Does not deter
Hypnotised, I stop and stare
The pinks, red, green, oranges
A night-time rainbow
Fireworks with no sound
The riot of colours, a calm without a storm
I have waited for you
My patience is rewarded
You came
I am blessed
Aurora
The Northern Lights.

Phoebe Matthews (16)
Hereford Cathedral School, Hereford

My Rainbow

Angry red that's when I have to clean out the shed,
Sunset orange that's when I eat porridge
Sunny yellow that's when I feel so mellow,
Pea-green that's when I have a nice dream,
Sky blue that's when I eat tiramisu,
Peachy pink that's when I'm on an ice rink,
Incredible indigo that's when I make cookie dough

All of these things are special to me,
But you'll find them too in life just wait and see.

Evie Jones (11)
Hereford Cathedral School, Hereford

Always Check For Fake News

F or real, not everything you see is true
A lways check twice before you
K ickstart on about some fake news
E ach one of you should always check before you lose

N egligent, are the people who catch you out
E ven try to scam you, so don't let them knock you out
W herever, whatever you see on the internet
S o always remember to check twice, so don't forget to not fall into their net.

Charlie Fowler (12)
Hereford Cathedral School, Hereford

No Filters

I want to see the real you
Not the fake, photoshopped
Filtered you.

I want the unaltered
Genuine you. Even if
That is misguided
And uncomfortable.

All the unobtainable, perfect people
Make us ourselves
And lose ourselves in their
Patronising lies.

Escape the likes and swipes
Follow your own path
And write your own story.

Don't hide the truth inside!

Izzy Early (12)
Hereford Cathedral School, Hereford

Sprinting For Gold

S printing ahead, wind running through my world
P ushing my limits, leaving fears behind
R acing with friends, heart beating fast
I love the rush, nothing can compare
N ever giving up, I run after gold
T he end is in sight as I sprint for my life
I cannot go on without a fight
N ear, so near, I fight to my death
G old or nothing as I take my last breath.

Elodie Alcott (13)
Hereford Cathedral School, Hereford

Love Is My Truth

It's something warm and mythical,
A magic force that is invisible.
It's an unimaginable, special miracle,
It's eternal and immortal but not visible.
It's a sense of hope, a feeling of wonder,
It's a tingle of electricity, a calming thunder.
It's something that makes you warm inside,
A lovely sensation that makes you satisfied.
So in a world where you can be anything, be kind.

Artie Jackson (11)
Hereford Cathedral School, Hereford

Brutal Leaders

Money is what charities are needing,
But good destiny is what people are seeking,
All brutal leaders burn,
Yet never do they learn,
They just can't see,
But their followers agree,
Still, they don't mind
That there are people still to find,
All they do is bomb and bomb,
And act as if nothing's wrong,
People starving in the night,
Soldiers fight for what is right.

Emilia John (12)
Hereford Cathedral School, Hereford

Be Real In The Fake World

Others stroll past it,
Carelessly leaving it,
Waiting for the next
Person to fall over it.

In their eyes,
The world is gloomy
All the joy removed,
The world feels roomy.

When I go past it,
I pick it up,
Putting it in the bin,
Helping the planet with a win.

In my eyes, the
World gets more beautiful
And skies get brighter every time.

Clara West (13)
Hereford Cathedral School, Hereford

Truth Of The Waves

She was calm today
The waves lapped at my feet
The soft foam in-between my toes
The sun's face smiled through the reflection on the waves
Soaking the sky and sand in oranges and pinks.

She was fierce today
The waves crashed wildly against the dark rocks
The sharp salty air reddening my cheeks
Froth and spray filled the air
As gulls cried high in the bitter grey sky.

Esme Yorke (16)
Hereford Cathedral School, Hereford

Frozen In Time

Endless, stood before me
Fog surrounded me
Time stood still
Darkness, in which was it
The dead jagged limbs of the trees
Poked and prodded at me until
The hairs on the back of my neck
Stood up to attention
The fragmental bark crackled
And twisted until forever
Endless stood before me
Fog surrounded me
Time stood still
Darkness, in which was it.

Archie Gladwyn (11)
Hereford Cathedral School, Hereford

Fake Face

In our world where masks are the rage,
Where smiles are scripted on a fake stage.
I walk with the weight of what is true and sincere,
In a land drawn with shadows and fear.

The filters may smooth out lines on our faces,
But behind every image, a soul we should embrace.
So, I shake off the mask to let the colours go wild,
Embrace all my flaws, to be a curious child.

Mary Connop (15)
Hereford Cathedral School, Hereford

Is This Really What We Are Made For?

Is this really what we're made for?

We sit on our phones for four hours a day,
70 days a year, just chucked away.
Lost in endless scrolling,
Whilst time just keeps on rolling.

This idea needs to change,
Before it's too late.
Before we feed the next generation,
And put them in the same state.

Is this really what we are made for?

Ollie Yates (15)
Hereford Cathedral School, Hereford

Cheese

Oh, how I love a block of cheese
It does indeed fulfil my needs
I fill my face but Mother pleads
"Stop eating so much cheese
Lactose intolerance brings you to your knees."
I say, "But Mother, please
Without cheese, my heart bleeds
I will die
I'll be deceased
Then I shall have no more cheese
And only then will you be pleased."

Evelyn Davies (13)
Hereford Cathedral School, Hereford

The Game

The game of rugby is so great
Although it's one most people hate
It's the one for me and my mate

We pass the ball down the line
Coaches tell us we shine
This game is the best
It's better than the rest

This game is made for me
And it's called rugby
I get the ball and score a try
I finish it all with a match tea pie!

Ashley Wilson (12)
Hereford Cathedral School, Hereford

The False Truth

Lies create distance.
Shutting out the truth of who we are,
Building walls between us.
Turning lies into reality.

Opportunities are lost,
People become unheard,
Looks start to define us.
Turning assumptions into the truth.

The real story is forgotten,
Connections break.
Loyalty is lost,
This is the power of stereotypes.

Mimi Boniface (15)
Hereford Cathedral School, Hereford

Procrastination

S mall periods become longer ones
T ime that was yours becomes lost forever
O pened doors into the future close, continuing the cycle
L etters of commendation, prizes, grades, everything lost
E ven family, friends, the dearest things, put to the side
N ow is your time, it's not too late, put the phone down.

Jack Jones (15)
Hereford Cathedral School, Hereford

Internet

I nvisible bullying hides in the digital space
N ever-ending problems hiding behind a screen
T errifying results of online risk
E asily falling to silly scams
R isks of privacy invasion
N ever truly safe
E very click could lead you to danger
T rapped in a world of fraud and manipulation.

Monty Harrison (12)
Hereford Cathedral School, Hereford

Be Social

In the glare of screens
We lose the warmth of faces
Digital embrace. We lose the warmth of faces
Digital embrace.

Step outside, breathe deep
Nature's call, a gentle nudge
Hearts in sync, we meet.

Laughter fills the air
Moments shared, connections made
Life beyond the glare
Hearts in sync, we meet.

Daimen James (13)
Hereford Cathedral School, Hereford

Admiring It

Each day you can make a sandwich
And try to fill it with nice things
Why not make your day a sandwich,
And fill it with nice things

Strings of things that can make you sing
Sing with love and kindness
For this will, to others, bring
The gift of happiness

Look back on your day
And admire it.

Toby Baxter (12)
Hereford Cathedral School, Hereford

The Beautiful Truth

Truth is like a star
Always there
Wearing gold
Alone they are and
Silently they sit
And sometimes
They may shine
Until they die out
Eventually

Tucked in the deep blue
Hidden away
To be revealed by the darkest patch of sky
Unfolded to reveal something blinding
Blinding.

Emily Driver (15)
Hereford Cathedral School, Hereford

Our Precious World

In our world full of radiant flowers, busy bees,
Wild animals and the tallest trees;
Birds that sing such sweet melodies,
They are sacred in all our countries.

So why, oh why do we risk it all?
With oceans rising, and urban sprawl.
A layer of warmth growing like a fireball,
Now is the time to stop our world's downfall.

Arabella Clark (15)
Hereford Cathedral School, Hereford

Football

F orever dreaming, might it come true
O nly if you practice
O r if you don't, you might stagnate
T rying hard
B uilds confidence and strength
A bility to see the end goal
L onging for it to come true
L eads to the beautiful truth.

William Ingmire (12)
Hereford Cathedral School, Hereford

A School Summer

In a school a bell rings,
The start of summer is nearing,
The students all run past the hall
Classes shake, paintings fall
As the teachers open the gates
The children wait
They talk about the holidays
They are going to have
Suddenly there is a shout
As they all run out.

Mary Wardle (11)
Hereford Cathedral School, Hereford

Free In A Fake World

Screams silenced
Connections real
Nature whispers truths we feel
In digital deserts, we break the seal.
Fingers freed from pixel binds
We find our way through ancient signs
Under skies where freedom winds
Eyes open to the world untamed
Lives lived, our souls unchained.

Mylo Verrall-Bhasin (12)
Hereford Cathedral School, Hereford

Cautious

C areful of scams
A ware of fraud
U nless you're sure it's safe
T reat it with thought
I nside, there's spam
O utside, you're bored
U ntil you're ready
S tay safe online, don't get floored!

Toby Whitaker (12)
Hereford Cathedral School, Hereford

The Singing Thrill

S tanding on stage, feeling the thrill,
I n every note, I find my peace.
N otes soar high, emotions fly,
G iving my all, proud in the sound of my voice.
E choes of dreams fill the air,
R hythm and melody show I care.

Glasha Connolly (13)
Hereford Cathedral School, Hereford

Gaming

G aming is unhealthy for under-11s
A ddicting children and brainwashing them
M inds forgetting schoolwork
I ntelligence can fall through the floor
N ow it is time to put the controllers down and
G o outside!

Harry Buchanan (12)
Hereford Cathedral School, Hereford

Soldier

Four men in uniform to carry home my soldier,
As time flies by,
He grows colder,
As we put down flowers,
The memories of him develop more sour,
When he was little,
He dreamed of being a soldier,
There he is,
My little soldier.

Lola Wyatt (12)
Hereford Cathedral School, Hereford

Ambassador

- **A** brodietical
- **M** asterpiece
- **B** athysiderodromophobia
- **A** damantine
- **S** assy
- **S** elf-disciplined
- **A** dventurous
- **D** edicated
- **O** rganised
- **R** espectful.

Eleanor Huxtable (11)
Hereford Cathedral School, Hereford

Truthful

T elling people what is real
R ight thing
U nderstanding
T he truth
H appiness
F alse news
U sing people for the right thing
L iving with integrity.

Martha Powell (12)
Hereford Cathedral School, Hereford

A Perfect World

The perfect world is in the palm of our hands,
We've got the strength,
We've got the power,
We've got the kindness, most important of all,
All we've got to do is create it.

Barnaby West (11)
Hereford Cathedral School, Hereford

The Tree

One windy day, a tree,
Which was called Lee,
It grew and grew,
Sadly, it caught the flu,
But it was old and free.

George Hinton (12)
Hereford Cathedral School, Hereford

Be Yourself
A haiku

Be yourself right now
Don't change because of others
Don't let them change you.

Hunter Martin (12)
Hereford Cathedral School, Hereford

England
A haiku

Vast hills squat down low
Where once were lush woodlands now
Forts from fairy tales.

Matthew Hughes (13)
Hereford Cathedral School, Hereford

Don't Change
A haiku

The world is so cruel
Don't change yourself to fit in
You are amazing.

Ali Elrefaiy (13)
Hereford Cathedral School, Hereford

Being Real In A Fake World
A haiku

Always check for lies
Be truthful and check for scams
Always be careful.

Harry Crawford (12)
Hereford Cathedral School, Hereford

Pages Come Alive
A haiku

Pages come alive
Ink that tells an adventure
Musty aged fragrance.

Zachary Pepper-Wilby (12)
Hereford Cathedral School, Hereford

Questioning Reality

In this modern day
What should we class as real?
Am I even real?

Robin Hughes (15)
Hereford Cathedral School, Hereford

Cheap Flowers

Her green fluorescent eyes dance
across the room, a flurry of familiar
faces, barely focused in frame, fling
unforgotten phrases at her. Eyes,
darting everywhere to locate some form of
escape - alas, nothing is retrieved. She
weeps without crying and lets out a
small but subtle smile - enjoyment? No,
of course not. Inside, a pool of sorrow
harbours resemblant terms; how
has the surface tension not broke?
How indeed. Her eyes, ears, mouth: worth no more
than £1.99.

She misplaces herself, wandering
around the enclosure she is trapped in.
She sighs, gazing at intimate strangers;
they fling different but equally powerful
lexis at her, unrelenting. However,
one individual ceases for a moment; escape?
She desperately struggles over to receive
a glimpse of freedom. A way out?
The individual hands them a small gift
before continuing the onslaught. A prize
worth no more
than £1.99.

One deadly step in the wrong direction
leaves her stranded, alone, helpless in the open.
They stare, look, and gaze with little point and pity;
She squints, turns away with reason and sorrow.
Before eyes are shut, she glimpses
towards a stem; a flower, a lotus.
Glancing at the tag: £1.99.
Staring into the pool below it, a murky depth.
How has such a lifeform prospered? She
admires its beauty and resilience. She
smiles, for if a flower could, why couldn't she?
Standing, because a flower can, and she can, too.
Steadfast, as she is worth much more
than £1.99.

Moon Carr (18)
Highfields School, Matlock

Anxiety

I feel the creature again, whispering in my ear,
Growing and feeding my biggest fear.
It moves to my heart, making it beat painfully fast,
I try to distract myself 'til the feeling has passed.
It's now 1am and the creature's got louder,
I'm at my weakest, well, it's just getting prouder.
Uncontrollable tears are being dragged down my face,
The creature's growing, filling up the whole place.
My head has gone light but my swollen eyes ache,
I need someone's help but there's no one awake.
The crying has started to make me feel sick,
Me fighting this creature's like a feather versus brick.
I reach under my pillow and pick up my phone,
It's now 2am, no one will answer, so I'm truly alone.
I'm scared of myself and how fast my heart's beating,
I push off my covers because I'm overheating.
I try all my techniques, breathe in and breathe out,
I start to feel like I am going to black out.
This panics me more and I start to shake,
This creature is bit by bit making me break.

Leila Brett (13)
Highfields School, Matlock

Dreams Matter

To be a vet is to be a dream,
Being a vet makes me seem
As though I'm in a dream.

Animals are my pride and joy,
Without animals, my life wouldn't be a joy.

Helping animals is a dream,
And seeing them happy is a dream.

If your animal is hurt or sick,
One day, I could help them be better,
But for now, it's just in my dreams,
That one day, I hope to achieve.

Some days, it seems as though you can't achieve your dreams,
But showing you that dreams matter
Could make you seem happier.

Lexi Robinson (13)
Highfields School, Matlock

Strength Of Scars

In the depths of hurt, where shadows weep,
a silent promise begins to sleep,
each throb and ache, a lesson learned,
through the pain, my strength is burned.
The body bares what the mind can't face,
through every struggle, we must find our pace,
dealing with the pain we're forced to embrace.
As muscles mend and scars lay low,
we gather strength from what we know.

Immy Rifkin (13)
Highfields School, Matlock

The Difference Of The Day And Night

Day or night, there is always a light,
White or black, there is always a guide,
Born or not born, there is always a life,
Day or night, there is always a sound,
Cat or dog, they are always on the ground,
Human or child, they always love pounds,
Doctor or not, there is always a hero,
Day or night, there is always a knight.
Night or day, there is always right.

Daniel Jellis (12)
Highfields School, Matlock

Things That I Dislike

Everyone likes different things, and people go to all sorts of places,
Everyone likes to enjoy different foods and go to lots of spaces.
But people also dislike many things, it makes people different,
The things that I don't like,
I hate crowded rooms, and my money spent,
I hate being too busy and having to do so many jobs in the house,
I hate little creatures like spiders, rats and mice,
I hate loud noises that rattle my ears and make me lose control,
I hate eating fruit and vegetables, I hate coal,
I hate chewy, creamy, crunchy foods,
I hate really tall dudes,
I hate being alone in the dark, I hate children playing in the park,
The sound of them shouting and screaming, the creaking of the old swing and the rubbing of the red slide.
I hate long car journeys and being bored,
I hate difficult lessons and having to use every part of my brain,
I hate hard games that make me rage and go insane,
But everyone is different and unique in their own special way,
And they all have the right to say

What they like and hate,
And speak to your mate,
That everything turns out in the end,
Just go round the bend.

Dylan James (17)
Laleham Gap School, Ramsgate

Agriculture Life

I am a farmer
I am 1 in 1000 people who are in agriculture
People think I have money but I am skint
I am like everyone, struggling with Brexit
I wish I had two pairs of hands but it is impossible
I am working 24-7 to help the economy every day
I am trying to make a profit every second of the day, whatever the weather is
I am still working, I cannot afford to just sit there
People think agriculture is easy but it is not
You have to fix things like maintaining a tractor
So it is not just sitting around all day because you cannot afford to
But we are still going to help the economy as it is just a normal day, whatever the day is
I am a farmer.

Henry Hoile (16)
Laleham Gap School, Ramsgate

Marmite

Marmite makes me happy.
Marmite smells nice.
Marmite, some people hate.
Marmite, some people love.
Marmite tastes good.
Marmite is unpredictable.
Marmite makes anything taste great.
Marmite is amazing.
Marmite.

Thurston Miles (16)
Laleham Gap School, Ramsgate

Art Is...

Art is very subjective.
A viewer could dismiss it in an instant or could love it for eternity
The pinky tones and striking blues might soothe the eye and tempt the wallet
Or
The colourblind might disregard the image and care about the story
it is very subjective

Art is beauty
Using the swish of a paintbrush and the flick of a pen, a multitude of emotions can be seen
The look of love can be created on canvas and last forever
And
The wondrous giggles of a toddler can be captured with just one photo
It is beauty

Art is an escape
Every person has a piece of work that they view and find comfort
A charcoal drawing of a pet might bring someone back to their childhood
Also
Reminding them of their uni days and relive that moment for just a second
It is an escape

Art is personal
Anyone can express their problems or joy with swirls of colour and smears of paint
A love for a person so powerful, they cannot use words
So
They put it down on canvas and no one will know what they are really thinking
It is personal

People are art
They are subjective in every way, for it is impossible to be liked by everyone
They are beautiful characters who laugh, smile and cry
They are an escape for someone to talk to and love
They are personal individuals.
People are art.

Mima James (14)
Monkton Combe Senior School, Monkton Combe

Doodles

Struggling to focus
I can't help but turn and stare
Her doodles create smiles
And bring a sense of warmth in the air

Her drawings of orchids with different shapes and patterns
Flood the page with her heart and soul
She draws with confidence and experience
Like a natural-born artist, but hiding away in a hole

It makes my mind twist and turn
These flowers make me stop and think
If there is a deeper meaning hiding away
Or maybe I'm starting to overthink

I build up the courage to ask her
Why the flowers she draws are always orchids
Her hand stops as she turns to face me
I could see the water about to gush out of her eyelids

They are for my mother
She says to me
Like a vulnerable puppy
Her eyes swell up nervously

She lost her mother not long ago
A graceful and kind woman; the opposite of arrogant
A beautiful orchid tree lay always in her garden
So keeping her orchids alive on her page is the most important

Struggling to focus
I can't help but turn and stare
Her doodles create smiles
And bring a sense of warmth in the air.

Anouk Chioke (14)
Monkton Combe Senior School, Monkton Combe

She

If they were a boy,
They would be excused
From the dirt dragged in,
Through the living room

If they were a boy,
They wouldn't be shunned
For the pictures they post
Whilst tanning in the sun,
Bullied
Outcasted

If they were a young man,
They're assumed to be the boss
But they aren't young men.
They are told to be obedient,
They are told they are crazy if they get cross

If they were a man,
The bare minimum is respect
Whilst leading their meeting with coffee down their shirt
Hair in a mess, stressed, stupid mess, upset
This can't be real
But
With irritating, discriminatory respect

If they were a man,
They would be taken seriously

Their murder wouldn't be an 'accident',
Their life is more precious, it seems
As women live in fear, solidarity
Terror.

Two million women
Every year

We are frigid when we say no,
We are easy if we say yes.
We are too big for our britches if we are educated on a subject,
We are dumb when we don't understand.

What if she were your daughter?
Your aunt? Your mum? Your role model?
You'd understand
If she were a man.

Faith Karamura (14)
Monkton Combe Senior School, Monkton Combe

The Canvas

We all have a brush
The day we are born
It gets to work
Painting.

Each decision we make
Road we take
Cake we bake
And morning we wake
Adds to the canvas that once was…

Blank.

Blank no more
The dark days turn the paint vibrant
The light turn the paint grey
This happens until you see
The truth.

Each hue tells a story
Each line a refrain
Laughter, sorrow, joy and pain
The art of existence in layers displayed.
And the day we open our hearts…

The truth is unveiled
When the colour inverts
When each brush stroke holds a lifetime
When we reside in the present

And grow from the past
When we decide what defines us
And what landscape is ours

So in the gallery on life
And the archive of time
Your tapestry will hang
Next to theirs and by mine.

Just remember for next time
When you're given a canvas
Paint on it what you will
But remember each mark is forever.
There is no turning back through time.

Amber Ashman
Monkton Combe Senior School, Monkton Combe

Could There Be Hope?

Injustice
Segregation
Slavery
Pain

Fighting
Conflict
Grief
Racism

This is the reality of many today
Pain, fear, hopelessness, defeat

Being spat at
And stared at
Faces pulled at them
Racist comments said to their faces

What has the world become?

Think about our heroes
Martin Luther King Jr
Rosa Parks
Roy Wilkins
Thurgood Marshall

They fought for what's right
And died for our rights

But
At what cost?

The foot on the neck
A black man's neck
Sent the world into anger
As he cried his last words

"I can't breathe."

So could there be hope?
A glimmer of hope shining through the cracks
The cracks of hatred, suffering and pain

Our ancestors fought
And we should fight too
Fight for our rights, for unity
Fight for our freedom.

Ashley Fai
Monkton Combe Senior School, Monkton Combe

Still The Same, I Can't See, Can You?

I thought it was alright

Really hoped they wouldn't try

The irony, after all this time,
all these places,
all these faces and all those gateways of guilt,
but all your face says is help.

So no,
It's really not alright,
and calling out isn't right.

I push it away.
It comes back.

Now this stress has you falling apart.

They undermine,
line for line
or more time flying while you're
still stuck trying to find
the same words to rehearse
but.

You might find.

That no, it never works,
and yes, they're

always
worse.

Stop

Think

Realise

It's alright

Have faith,
faith in your words,
faith in your face,
faith that whenever you step, the floor won't go.
Have faith in your
faith

Yet I don't in mine.

Rufus Difazio (14)
Monkton Combe Senior School, Monkton Combe

Crash Ball

Whistle blows
Time slows
Thud of studs
Boots in the mud

Here's the prop
Make him stop
Drop a shoulder
Down with that boulder

Ball is out, I hear the call
Pick it up, run at the wall
Make a break and say goodbye
Off I go to score a try.

The winger's down, I shattered his head
Come on mate, it's not like you're dead
I've passed the ball, I catch it and run
I say to defenders, "Sit down, you're done."

Final whistle blows. Collisions all over
Scoreline echoes like a supernova
No more tackles for me to seek
That's okay, repeat next week.

Walter Wheeler
Monkton Combe Senior School, Monkton Combe

The Watcher Of The Sea

Salty waves crash down upon the sand
Then slowly creep up the beach.
She sits and watches this happen -
Over and over again
A cold statue who got caught up
And lost in the moment.

Early morning sunlight reflects off of her metal body
And bounces off into the ocean
Dancing atop white-capped waves -
Diving deep down
Where the statue cannot quite see.

Whilst the waves will always roll up and down the beach
She will be there to watch them.

Ana Champion (14)
Monkton Combe Senior School, Monkton Combe

Summer's Absence

Summer, O' summer, O'
Where have you gone?
You fled without saying,
Have I done you wrong?

Sunshine, O' sunshine, O'
Why must you cloak?
When all you do is
Isolate me
Out here to soak?

Rain, O' rain, O'
Why must you fall?
When I to you
Have done nothing at all?

Green, O' green
Why must you fade?
Now all the leaves
Have all decayed.

Summer, O' summer
Please grant my request
I long for you back
Do you really need to rest?

Jayden Swanston (15)
Monkton Combe Senior School, Monkton Combe

Why Are You Still Watching?

A red car is parked nearby.
As a tank rolls passed.
A crow flies in the sky
But the planes caused a blast.
And we just watch.

Little green men rush forward
As a nearby building collapses.
They fight to gain reward
But after months, they begin to relapse.
And we are still watching.

Streets littered with corpses.
Even those who didn't fight.
Explosions occur but not military forces
In a war, you can lose all your rights
And we are still watching.

These politicians may shake hands
But we'll never get their demands
We may one day have peace
But that may be impossible to reach.
Yet we are still watching.

Denis Rimeikis (13)
New College Leicester, Leicester

Nigeria

We are Nigeria,
We are known for our delicious and varieties of food,
With a bite and taste of our food
You will be moved.

Suya, suya, suya
A delicious taste, which can control your mind
Heart and soul
The spiciness of it, the grills of it
Can never be understood
Enjoyed in the night with garri or bread,
Watching a movie or playing a game
Suya, suya, suya

Some people say we are poor
But with an eye to see us
We are rich and well-developed
We are educated but not employed,
But if we can change our lives
We would be a better person in future.

Green, white, green
Green is for life,
Green is our colour, green is who we are
Though we fall several times
But one day, we will rise.

We never give up, we stay together, brave and strong
Even though life is tough
We are tougher than life itself
Like the plants that come alive after
Being burnt,
We remain evergreen.

Nigeria's culture is incredibly rich and diverse
Over 250 ethnic groups and more than 500 languages,
The major ones,
Igbo, Yoruba, Hausa
With its unique customs, languages
And artforms.

The Yoruba's agbada, the Igbo's isi agu,
The Hausa's Baban Riga
Showcasing intricate designs and patterns
Green is for agriculture
And we remain green.

Harmony Uwujare (14)
New College Leicester, Leicester

The Clock

I stare at the clock, immersed in thought
Thinking about thoughts
What thoughts?
Sad thoughts, happy thoughts?
It feels like I'm floating in space
Floating in thought.
What is the teacher talking about?
I wouldn't know, I'm in thought.
My mind skipping from world to world.
What am I going to grow up to be?
What is life about?
Am I going to make it to see my grandkids when I'm old?
Thoughts clicking in my head
Like the clicking of a clock.
I'm in outer space, then the bell goes.
Suddenly, I'm back on Earth, looking at the clock,
I go on with my day and forget all my thoughts.

Yannis Dorobantu (13)
New College Leicester, Leicester

A Woman Of Colour? No A Woman Of Rights!

School tells you to live life to the fullest,
but how can you do that if people are racist?
If you have a darker complexion,
the world will give you a free lesson.
The back of the bus is not a seat to discard
the people society says are different from us
as if we're trying to hang them on drying racks.
Do you ever feel like you're shackled
by chains that are gripping at your veins?
Well, try being black for a day.
Ready to get sent to the back of the bus
for just showing your skin colour?
Well, people like Rosa Parks are just like us.
So, what's the fuss about the way she looks?

Ivie Saddler (13)
New College Leicester, Leicester

Deception

Once upon a long, long time
A boy named Jack; he was sublime.
But he surrendered to his gruelling fate
The person behind that screen
He was two-faced.
He never actually got to know him
But he can tell you now, he should've.
Lies, deception and deceit
That is not a good thing, possibly.
"But what can I do?"
That is my life
What he says is good and true.
But spilling out all the beans
Gets him up from his knees.
Learning how to tell
A friend or foe
Oh yes, that makes you grow.

Onyx Onyekwere (11)
New College Leicester, Leicester

War - Longing For The Past

I walk down the street of my old home,
Realising I'm on my own,
No mum, no dad,
Just regrets that make me feel bad.
Missing being in their warm arms,
Just to see one on the pathway without being alarmed.
It's not something new to me,
It's just something I now see.
Rubble flooding the grounds,
I fear I hear no sounds.
Life used to be of laughter and glee,
Now I wish to not be.
Ashes fill my lungs,
As I try to speak with a tired tongue.

The aftermaths of war.

Hafsat Sulaiman (14)
New College Leicester, Leicester

Children In The Darkness

The darkness submerges our eyes,
Day by day, we tell our children goodbyes.
Don't let the darkness fill our eyes,
Scared to let your kids go out at night,
We don't know what dangers are ready to bite.
Not knowing when they're coming back.
Staying cautious and keeping our guard up,
Reports on the missing every day on the news,
Whilst the police go search for clues.
By the end of the investigation, their focus, dead.
Now the coffin in the grave is their new bed.

Rhuben Glover (13)
New College Leicester, Leicester

Consent

Consent is key if you want to be with me.
It's a yes or no, not a maybe.
If it's a yes, yes, we'll open the door,
If it's a no, it's a danger zone.
Remember this beat and don't be a creep.

Consent is good,
Do you know what this means?
I can tell you what it means,
Consent, sincerity, getting permission,
Yeah, yeah, yeah.

Get consent, be exceptional,
Noteworthy, wondrous, pleasant,
Not heinous, odious, horrendous.

Travaee Pearson (11)
New College Leicester, Leicester

Social Media

Why are children nowadays so manipulated?
Why are children nowadays so influenced?
I will tell you why
Social media

Bullying, deception and lying
Speaking from my heart, I'm telling you
Loss of self-confidence
Insecure with your appearance

We need to take action
Or children in future years
Are going to only listen to
These delusions.

Amelia Pitijeva (13)
New College Leicester, Leicester

The Things Social Media Can Do

Social media can lead to the worst
And also the best, but not everything
Can be how it seems...
You see, people tend to use filters on themselves
To get fame and likes
But beauty isn't always the way to fame
It's about the way you act
And live your life, instead of being manipulated.
So don't let people choose who you are
Just be yourself.

Janiah Semedo (11)
New College Leicester, Leicester

Chicken Nugget

Chicken, chicken nugget,
Over the hills and far away,
The chicken nugget comes out to play.
It tastes amazing with chips
And even better with dips!
Oh, the appearance is amazing.
Just looking at it, my mouth is salivating.
If you take the chicken nuggets from me,
My rage will be like a bear
And trust me, the fight won't be fair.

Joseph Mulroy (12)
New College Leicester, Leicester

I Won't Write A Poem

The cat wore a hat
There, that's that!
I'm not going to make this rhyme
Because that would be a waste of time.
I won't use alliteration
Because my boredom would be a big, bad situation
I won't use a simile because it's a bother
And it would make my emerald-like eyes water.
And I won't... wait -

Paulina Jokubauskyte (12)
New College Leicester, Leicester

Deception

D on't let social media fool you.
E verything is fake
C orruption is filled around there.
E specially trolling, bullying
P eople judging your appearance
T rying hard to deceive you
I llusions all around
O verconfidence is down to the floor
N ever trust social media.

Amira Moon (13)
New College Leicester, Leicester

Social Media Is A Lie

Your confidence is gone
Your trust is gone
But why?
Social media is a lie
Instagram models
Magazine models
Stop with your delusion
It is all an illusion.
The generations to come
Are going to give in to the deception
Of social media.
I'm telling you this with sincerity
Social media is a lie!

Hollie Wain McCabe (13)
New College Leicester, Leicester

Bullied

B ullied because I'm beautiful
U seless feelings, sadness, pain
L ook at me, I am not dull
L ook at me, I am the same
I ndividual, identity and illusion
E veryone is different. Please stop the pain
D on't bully me. It causes confusion for my beautiful brain.

Hollie Hirons (11)
New College Leicester, Leicester

Mental Feelings

Mental feelings are hard
To make them, to feel them.
Differences, different people,
Anxiety, depression and anger.
Deep down inside, you will cry it out
At night. Don't be scared, just find it out,
Cry out loud.
Just dance around and have a blast.
Just remember these feelings will never last.

Phoebe Coles (11)
New College Leicester, Leicester

Bullying

Such a tragedy that reminds us of history
You get teased like a Malteser
So harsh sometimes you get a rash
Bruises, cuts and grazes from all the pushing
Kicking, punching
It's as if I'm crunching
Your mind shatters into pieces like matter
The silence is loud
Making a sound.

Fidelis Appiah (12)
New College Leicester, Leicester

In A World Which

War is a never-ending fight between us, ourselves and our world.
In a world which...
A million other men, women and children have to die for our hatred.
In a world which...
Red blood is on our hands, as we go unaware with our day ungratefully.

Mariam Shamsaddin (11)
New College Leicester, Leicester

Food

Chicken bucket, chicken nugget
Large fries, pumpkin spice
Milkshake, earthquake
Big Mac, big stacks
Full meal, major deal
Taste to my knees of cheddar cheese.

Caden Flattley (13)
New College Leicester, Leicester

Identity

Deleting an old app is like a flower descending off the branch.
Downloading a new app is like a flower blossoming out of the branch.
By winter, blossoms rot.

Honya Fuad (13)
New College Leicester, Leicester

Olympics

Sprinting down the track
In a very fast pack
Swimming down the pool
In a one-on-one duel
The Olympics is here
Don't shed a tear.

Freddie Burdett (14)
New College Leicester, Leicester

Climate Change

C ars are sending out toxic fumes,
L ife in the sea is heading to its doom,
I n this chaos, we all decide
M odern life is worth the ride.
A ll the trees are coming down,
T owns by the sea are beginning to drown,
E cosystems are beginning to die.

C hange has a chance but we don't try,
H appy lives will come to an end,
A ll the oceans, our rubbish, we send,
N o more icebergs will remain,
G uys, this is a problem, not a game,
E arth is dying and nobody cares,
S o help the Earth and answer our prayers.

Kaitlyn Doyle (11)
Penrice Academy, St Austell

Not All Men

Women have tried it all,
We tried pepper spray and switchblades,
We tried not leaving the house once the sun fades,
We tried alarms and whistles and safety apps,
We tried sending our location through Google Maps,
We tried sticking together, always in pairs,
Avoiding things like Uber, the train, the bus, the stairs,
We covered up our shoulders, chest, legs and butts,
We tried being polite, never making a fuss,
We tried saying no,
They said it a million times,
But he believed forcing them wasn't worthy of a crime,
Why is the burden always on us women?
They'll say, "If you didn't want it to happen, then why'd you let in him?"
We've changed our behaviours, our mindset, our strength,
But when we ask men to help, most won't go the length,
We're asking for your support, so please tell us
When you'll stop replying to our pain by saying, "Not all men."
More concerned with our tone than what we actually have to say,
And I hope to God it doesn't happen to a woman you love, one day,
We know it's not all men, but it's too many of us,
And all we are asking is for you to be men we trust!

Please listen to our pain, listen to our voices,
We need men to start changing, we've run out of other choices.

Caja Dowrick (11)
Penrice Academy, St Austell

Wonderful World

W ake up!
O ur world is dying.
N o longer can we ignore the facts.
D on't just sit there scrolling, let's act!
E xplore why our sea levels are rising.
R iots rage across the world.
F ree our world from droughts and heat waves.
U nderstand the damage we are causing.
L iving creatures face extinction.

W eather systems are all changing.
O ur actions have consequences.
R educe, reuse and recycle.
L et's make a change.
D efend our planet for future generations.

Seren Thompson (11)
Penrice Academy, St Austell

Romantic

Know that my heart shall beat for you, even after death
Because nobody can express the way I feel about you even in the dark
I shall always be loving you as long as you are
Because I love you and nothing can ever change that, my love
Because I can always trust you, even if they have to kill me
I will never give in because I love you and trust you for infinity and nothing will ever change that.

Charlie Chesterfield (11)
Penrice Academy, St Austell

My Favourite Sport

My favourite sport is football.
I love to play it with my friends.
Football is so much fun.
We run fast and kick the ball
Into the goal.
Scoring a goal makes me
Happy!
I also enjoy watching football
Games on TV.
I cheer for my favourite team (Arsenal)
When they win, I'm really excited!

Keyaan Patel (11)
Penrice Academy, St Austell

Horses

H orses are amazing
O ften naughty
R eally cuddly
S illy and smart
E very horse is different
S mall or large in size.

Mollie Lee Baxter (11)
Penrice Academy, St Austell

A False Reality

Millions of photos are posted every day,
All looking exactly the very same way,
The same pose, the same smile,
No one's been unique in a while...

Fake looks and fake smiles,
You only show what you want us to see,
Why can't society let us be free?
I'm hiding behind a filter,
But I just want to be me,

Look at her - she looks amazing,
Why can't I look like her?
My face isn't as pretty,
And I haven't got her curves,

My looks, I don't like them,
I don't want them to be mine,
I think my friends are starting to hate me,
Because all I do is whine,
If only 'doctoring' was a crime.

Once you start, it's hard to stop,
If only we could turn back the clock
To a time when photos were real,
And appearance wasn't a big deal,

If I had one wish, one dream
Or something to hope for,

I'd wish for phones to not have screens anymore,
No 'selfies'; no filters; no editing at all,
Where we celebrated imperfections and
Embraced it all.

R Stephenson (14)
Pinderfields Hospital PRU, Wrenthorpe

Feels On Wheels

I stand here, at the foot of the ramp,
Thinking if I should do it.
The butterflies fly rapidly in my stomach,
My legs start to jiggle like jelly,
Overthinking about what injuries could occur.
"Sshh, relax your mind and do it!"

The wheels start rolling as I pick up speed,
It's relaxing as the wind blows in my face.
Boom!
A pebble.
I fall face first.
Like any obstacle in life, I must get back up,
But I don't.
I start shaking as I get up as the blood
Spirals through my body.
The embarrassment on my face.
I run back to my friend, we both laugh
At each other's 'fails'.

Whoosh.

A skater goes by doing the most insane trick
And landing all of them.
"Oh no."
Pebble.
Thump!
He falls...

But rolls back up like an Armadillo
It didn't even phase him at all...

This is a lesson in life we must learn:
Never give up and always try
No matter whether the challenge is high.

S Ali
Pinderfields Hospital PRU, Wrenthorpe

Live Or Live

Life is beautiful
Life is horrible
Life is tricky
Life is easy

We all have these views on life
It may not be in a close period, but it happens
You probably hate feeling so 'sensitive'
But it's beautiful how deeply you feel your emotions

You've likely had a time in your life where it feels like the end
But only you can change your view
Only you can put yourself in a better position
Would you believe me if I told you a flower could bloom in a dark room?

Everybody's journey is different
Life is like a train, you slow down, you speed up
Sometimes, another train could get in your way
But that doesn't mean you can't arrive at your destination.

F McCulloch
Pinderfields Hospital PRU, Wrenthorpe

Sails Adrift In Unrequited Tides Of Love

A tall sail sways in the sea air
The tides quietly move with the wind.
The boat adrift in far scapes of the vast sea
The boat is moving but it never
Truly sails the sea of love.
The sails are up but never moving with
The surroundings of the sea and sky.
The boat is moving but never truly ever moving.
The sea is moving around the boat
The sea birds can see from every angle from the skies
The potential and power of the boat.
The boat just never wanted to move further on
From where it was.
The other boat in the far sea sways closer to the boat
But never close enough to ever make the
Other boat sail its sails.

Janna Greer (15)
Slemish College, Ballymena

Refugees

Rain falls on my head,
Metallic taps on the roof above.
Pounding, shaking, lightning strikes.
You say I don't belong, I know I don't.
My muffled screams, silenced by the city lights.
I yearn to be freed from this trap.
Take me to where I belong.

Walls creeping with ivy,
Smothered in messages telling us to leave.
Don't you ever
Dare to come back.
I was told we would be welcomed,
Indulged in compassion.
But when I turn around,
All I see are the people who laugh and stare,
Mock me for my tear-stained face.
Take me to where I belong.

Everyone says they're kind, considerate, caring,
Until it comes to the point to express those traits.
Pointing, calling, laughing become the norm, like swarms of flies,
That 'kindness' as they call it.
Makes shivers
Run
Down my spine.

I make my hopeless pleas to
Take me where I belong.

If that is kindness, I am evil.

Questions circle my head,
How to fit in, how to be cool,
They tell us all not to change,
That you have to be true to yourself,
That they will like us for who we are,
But how can you do that if you're surrounded by the same plastic dolls?

My muffled screams, silenced by the odd remarks.
Take me to where I belong.

Marta Ossowska (14)
Slemish College, Ballymena

I Am Me And You Are You

People used to laugh as I walked by
But it never took my sunny smile.
People call me smart
But it can indeed be hard
Living up to people's hopes and thoughts
But I had to remember happiness cannot be bought.
Remembering this ignited
A fire that made my life brighter.

And don't forget
That I will never be you
And you will never be me
Because you will always be you
Like how I will always be me.

Joel Hagan (13)
Slemish College, Ballymena

Alfie

My foolish four-legged pup,
Jumping cheerfully up.
He's the most energetic boy,
Chasing us for his toy.

My little bright-eyed dog,
Who devours his food like a hog.
He is the most playful soul,
Running around for his ball.
He is like sunshine, clearing away the fog.

Paulina Ossowska (12)
Slemish College, Ballymena

Who Am I?

Who am I?
My mum says...
I am annoying, am I?
I am rude, am I?
I am cheeky, am I?
I am hyper, am I?
I am lazy, am I?
I am foolish, am I?
I think...
I am funny... maybe?
I am musical... maybe?
I am friendly... maybe?
I am persistent... maybe?
I am honest... maybe?
I am empathetic...?
Mrs Hoyland says I am irritating! Really?
Why fit in when you were born to stand out?

Tayyab (11)
The Elland Academy, Leeds

What Do I Believe?

I believe no one is all bad
I believe rules are meant to be broken
I believe you must keep trying
I believe pineapple on a pizza is mint!
I believe that you should stand out
I believe you must be brave
I believe you must dream big!
I believe my mum's Oreo cheesecake is the best thing ever!

Benji Remmer (12)
The Elland Academy, Leeds

I Am Who I Am

I believe I am polite
I believe I am fair
I believe I am funny and moody
I am ambitious and thoughtful
No one is all bad
I was born original and knowledgeable
I love travelling but I am sensitive.

Ellis Rockliffe (13)
The Elland Academy, Leeds

Made Of Glass

I am made of glass.
Treat me harshly and I will *smash*.
They see right through me all time round,
To this lifestyle, I am bound.
I'm here and there, I'm everywhere,
Though no one really seems to care.

They look right past me,
And pay attention to 'more important things',
But if they looked closer
They would see that I was *glittering*.
I'm made of glass but I'm not clear,
Inside holds something precious and dear.

Did you know how much there was to see?
Just open your eyes and *look at me*.
Do not glance or look straight through.
I wish you could see *me* the way I see *you*.

I do not want this glass skin,
I want something *real*, something *seen*.

Florence Morris (13)
Thomas Telford School, Telford

New Beginnings

Started a new school today, such a scary change,
Not sure where to go, all the classrooms looked strange.
I missed my old friends as I fondly pondered back,
"Come on, Eva! Get stuck in and give new things a crack!"

On the first day, I stepped through the gates,
Slowly but surely, I made some new mates.
Now my nerves have gone, it's time to learn the curriculum,
I must work hard and do more than the minimum.

I know I can do this, so I put on a big grin,
I start to feel comfortable and proud in my own skin.
I don't know why I felt so exposed and so scared,
It's a worry I guess, that all Year 7s have shared.

Eva Ligori (11)
Thomas Telford School, Telford

A Child's Dream

We've all had dreams,
Whether big or small;
Achievable or not,
We have all had them.

Mine was to fly.
No matter how or when,
I wanted to fly;
But fear flowed through my dreaming veins.

Yet, my delicate dreams were omnipotent;
And then I met Lilly.
Together, an unbreakable bond was formed that day;
One that carried on.

1, 2, 3, 4;
Flight!
And then, amazement,
I did it; it's possible
If mine is possible, then is yours?
As long as you believe,
You will achieve.

Kaitlan Astill-Evans (13)
Thomas Telford School, Telford

Life At Its Finest

The bees are buzzing,
The trees are whirling,
Life at its finest.
The leaves are stunning,
The air swirling,
Life at its finest.
Now, how could a time like this be greater?
The seasons change quickly; it's like a life changer.
Atmospheres around us change in a flash;
It's almost like they're in a rush.
The grass swaying
The leaves falling; autumn is here already
Soon it shall be winter; that much I know
We must be excited about the upcoming snow
This is life at its finest.

Luis Reeves (12)
Thomas Telford School, Telford

Dreams

How I live is how I am
I try to show them who I can be
But I am me and that's how I am always meant to be
Never let go of your dreams
You are you and you can be one of the best in a lot!

Seerat Maan (11)
Thomas Telford School, Telford

Taken

Who was that boy?
He had already been taken by a wave.
And was knocked out cold on the sea.
Like he was a feather being pulled in every direction,
Entering the endless pit of saliva.

Kasper Johnson (13)
Thomas Telford School, Telford

The World In Me

I have seen the world in me,
But some don't agree.

I was young, scared and shy.
I was scared to get in trouble, and I did not know why.
I started to write to set things straight,
Where my words of love will overcome hate.

I felt more pushed at the age of ten,
When I moved to another school, near my writing den.
I wanted to see more of the world,
I wanted to be that unique girl.

So I stood out, and wrote without decline,
I even started to sing in my spare time,
But I still stayed happy, until primary had ended,
And secondary is smooth, and my troubles have now mended.

I have seen the world in me,
And it's okay to disagree,
Don't feel shy to speak out,
We can understand what your concerns are about.
Teachers, parents, and classmates too,
Are always there to help you,
Let your dreams run wild until they suddenly erupt,
Love yourself, and never give up.

Jessica Shokanbi (11)
Townley Grammar School For Girls, Bexleyheath

Your Supernova

There is a Greek myth that says everybody has an other half,
One that is meant for them,
One that will compliment them in every single way,
Their soulmate in a sense.

I like to think that when these two people meet
There is an instant sense of belonging,
Like finding a part of yourself in someone else,
That is what happened when I found you.

My life that used to seem worth nothing suddenly became everything to me,
Because I discovered the beauty of a person's soul,
A soul that can bring colour to a monochromatic life,
A soul that made me feel safe,
A soul that seemed to speak to my very own.

It seemed like a silly story to me,
Finding someone to love,
But you proved me wrong,
And with that, I became happier.

But I was young then,
So maybe I was encapsulated by the thought of my first love,
The one which everyone wants to last,
But most of the time, it won't.

Because you see,
Whilst your soul was beautiful,
Like a supernova,
Mine was broken like a worn-out star,

Whilst you were my everything,
I was your something,
And finally, once my soul had seemed to heal and be rid of its weary state,
Yours had only seemed to grow tired around me.
Which is why when you left,
I broke.

My soul stopped singing,
It returned to its weary state,
And I was so confused.

Because you see,
The Greeks had a concept that everyone has an other half,
And I really thought you were mine.

And yet,
Even now that we are apart,
We seem to be interconnected,
We remember, we care and are never fully gone from each other,

That is why if I was to have a soulmate,
I would want it to be you,

As the darkness inside me has become brighter,
And my soul still sings for yours,

But even though I was younger then,
I am still young now,
And I would make the same choice every single time,
To fall in love with you,
Because your supernova healed my weary star,
Making it shine once more.

So maybe I am correct,
And you are that other half,
Or maybe I am wrong,
And you are not,

But I will wait and see because
The Greeks believed everyone had another half
And I think you might be mine.

As now my soul is like a supernova,
Just like yours.

Isabella French-Compagnoni (15)
Townley Grammar School For Girls, Bexleyheath

Avignon

The cliché sticks its tongue out, joker
young, blonde, ponytail-on-a-mission
Late at night and streetlights, they don't reveal it, not enough.
Grabbed, pulled, turned, and spat
out; it's not all but it's not any less.
There are truths that lurk like this at the knife's edge.
A sucked-in scream, hand-over-mouth sort of cover.
This story does not get old.
One keyboard slash away there are two worlds.
And they are writing your eulogy now.
He is
slick with sweat and hell's fire, for
the thrill of paper against muscle.
Back in the squeeze of the bustle
older, brown hair, sunglasses-can't-hide-it
The curtained courtroom reshuffle
what's a verdict if not her doom?
Three rooms built new, to hold the weight
of the blood and the sting
between the sheets when he leaves
the old stain stays
the old wound seeps.

Rosanna McNeil (17)
Townley Grammar School For Girls, Bexleyheath

That Which Surrounds Us

The beautiful truth -
A vague concept, which I cannot grasp.
For when I ponder on it for a simple moment,
Every ill, swarming thing beneath my skin flares up.

Upon further introspection:
Anger is simply successive over sadness
That it is inherent and inevitable - the yearn to break
Not merely that which is tangible

The truth that destruction has always
And will always be easier than creation
That your love is a fire destined to be a conflagration
Is that a beautiful truth?

That despite the aforementioned heat
You will regurgitate judgement and hate
Believed to be buried under the
Scorched soil inside of you.

(Is the beautiful truth a fallacy?
Are truths ever good?
Which great mind has ever been truly sane
Upon the discovery of 'truth'?)

Is the truth that one day, you'll stare at the floor wondering
If your heart has truly frozen over
However facing the stark reminder that
Our blood will still bleed warm, unkind red?

Red.

A colour, which I'm learning to be fond of;
It is the colour of my pet's eyes,
And the paint of the buses, which bring me to and from
A place where I feel more intensely than I ever have.

Perhaps there is a beauty in monotony,
Not everything important must be intense.
What joy is found in noise when true peace
Can be found in closed eyes and pillows?

In chirping birds and burrowing worms,
In poetry and art,
In the hum of wind when it's all too quiet,
In the people you will witness but never know.

Maybe the beautiful truth is that which surrounds us -
We are encompassed by beauty even when we fail to see it.
Though it's difficult to believe, there is beauty in everything,
Even in ourselves.

To me, the most beautiful truth is that:
Amongst everything ugly and dark within the mind,
Beauty can and will reach out to us,
We just must open our eyes to it.

Eva Matthew (15)
Townley Grammar School For Girls, Bexleyheath

The Brick Wall

We live in a world of uncertain times
Where trust is easily betrayed
Where people argue, scream, scratch
And the price is heavily paid

You know the world has gone terribly wrong
When friends turn against one another
When people gossip behind backs
Not caring for the feelings of the other

The world was once a solid wall
That stood without a crack
But slowly, we are tearing it apart
And discreetly trying to plaster it back

Plaster it back as it tears apart
As the cracks begin to spread
People try to cover up their mistakes
Rather than fixing them instead

It is the sad truth of the world we live in
As people would rather fix the wall
Than stop it from cracking in the first place
Which is a cost ever so small

But the wall, though filled with cracks
And damaged all around
Had started to grow a vine of roses
Starting from the ground

The vine of roses crept its way up
Covering up the cracks
Began to decorate the wall
Leaving beautiful roses in its tracks

And the wall, once greatly damaged
Turned into a colourful sight
And though it took lots of time
Turned into an amazing delight

Even when the world seems dark
As if painted in black
There will always be determined souls
Here to help turn it back

To a world filled with light and colour
Bright as ever could be
For people to stop and gaze in awe
At the world before them and see

And that is the truth of the world we live in
And a beautiful one at that
That even when everything is dark
Someone will be here to turn on the light.

Fire Depiver (11)
Townley Grammar School For Girls, Bexleyheath

From A Traveller In This Life

I am broken and beautiful, shattered yet stunning.
This world has shaped me for the worst;
Its talons crushed me;
And here I am, standing
Unwavered.
In my life short-lived
My eyes are shot with vermillion
Sights meant for those
Way beyond my years.
My heart has carried the burden
Of generations before me.
Slavery, discrimination, slander
Man betraying man
I have seen it all.
And yet, I grow
My spirit soars with wings
At times, it feels as if I am not present at all
Like a bird passing the horizon for the first time
And looking down at nature below him
As if I am an overseer of this life
A 'translucent wanderer'
I like to term myself.
And yet I watch
Ever patient
Waiting for Life's next move.
Waiting, waiting

For how Fate will trick me next
And where Destiny will lead me.
The truth
Is not appealing to look at;
The fact that it is so scarred, bruised, raw
Compiled of the hurt of every individual
Is what makes it beautiful.
The truth
Is beautiful because it is what
I live out.
My truth is me,
And I am beautiful,
All of my resilience and rage,
So therefore the truth is beautiful.

Michelle Fayoyin (15)
Townley Grammar School For Girls, Bexleyheath

Lyrico

January.
I blow out fireflies on sticks
they don't fall to their feet
my flesh hides inside a cotton frame
it's soft, and warm, and real.

There are rose petals in my hair
its thorns grow in my throat
while I make my 19th wish
they are thick and sharp and real.

I have wishes beyond your wildest dreams.
My wish is what keeps me moving
I've never loved somebody like you.
It's why I'm still here.
It's clear, and bold, and real.

August.
I leave my city for it
sell the fireflies for gold
I seal my thoughts in lead and pulp
because if I speak them, you'll leave
to someone who deserves you
I think it's one of the side effects
how could I deserve you?
You're wild, but sweet. You're not real.

December.
Tell me I'll understand...
It's not enough to understand.
You must love that about me.
Who are you to love me?
There are lyrics in my heart.
In a language my tongue rejects.
A language you reject.
I write it into my music, honey.
It's warm and sharp and real.

Comfort Adeyinka (16)
Townley Grammar School For Girls, Bexleyheath

The Beautiful Truth

A bloodthirsty pig
With an icy smile
Ears pricked up like a cactus
Rosy velvet-like cheeks
Dress as red as the sun
Boots as yellow as a lemon-flavoured gum
Covered in bronze mud
Quick feet moving towards me
Malevolent-looking face in front of me
Enormous pig licking its lips maliciously
As if saying to me, "Yes, I'll gobble down on you for a bit."
Oinks and snorts for a moment or two
Then calls over a friend
Who's a bit minute
My sudden gaze holds onto my eyes
Until I'm done staring
And take time to realize
Peppa Pig was in front of my eyes
Her and George, a big puddle they create
Then on the count of 3, they do a big jump
Making me gobble up a bucket of mud
Then I realise that I had mistaken them.
They just wanted to play
So playing with pigs
Is all that I did on that day
I still play with them now

At my old age
We jump in puddles
And eat Mummy Pig's noodles
A brilliant story
That I tell to this day
Because what you think of something
Could turn out to be your biggest mistake.

Victoria Esther Gilgal-Sale (11)
Townley Grammar School For Girls, Bexleyheath

Primary School

Don't talk about primary school
I used to just sleep and drool
The food... horrible
It was just so, so, so terrible
I swear I saw it moving
Stomp! Stomp! Stomp! Sorry, that was me running

It was technically a prison
It had us tied in like a ribbon
The people with Stanleys
They were the enemies
The Nativity play...
Let's just not talk about that day

I felt like a queen when I sat on those benches
While the others just looked like pigs eating in trenches
Miming the singing assemblies... always on the lookout
Ahhh... good old days, but if the teacher found out...
Hitting the person on the head in Duck Duck Goose
Oh, them... they just got the blues

Don't worry; this is the last verse
I need to hurry up because after this, I have to buy a new purse
What else... unsticking myself in Stuck in the Mud
I mean, nothing is wrong with that, it is not like I'm going to start a flood...

Rolling down your big socks into doughnuts
Rolling down your big school socks into doughnuts.

Iris Njomgang (11)
Townley Grammar School For Girls, Bexleyheath

Emotions

At first, my heart crashes
Out of my chest
My body collapses
And my palms sweat
Hot liquid drips
In swirling rings
From the top of my eyes
To the bottom of my chin

Then comes anger
In screaming lashes
Flames hurtle up
Amongst the ashes
My body is burning
My mouth is fuming
Everything explodes...
Debris... Silence

And suddenly happiness
Fills me up
It whooshes and floods
It flows down
Moving like the waves
Always remember there's a rainbow
Even when it rains

I dance, I shriek
I leap with delight

I gaze up at the stars
Ignited by moonlight
Happiness is something
That comes for free
The time wasted angry
Could be spent
Being happy

Emotions, make-up
Boys and girls
Without them
There would be something missing
From the world.

Harleen Mann (11)
Townley Grammar School For Girls, Bexleyheath

Be A Voice, Not An Echo

With a pencil, she draws on the chart
God, how doesn't she know she's smart?
Her smile glows
And my admiration grows
Her beauty is like a rose

Her giggles are the sunshine
Her pain is like the rain
We talk for ages - we almost never stop
We had so much in common - we almost never stop

She's like a star I try to reach
After a while, I start to beseech
You slip out of my hands like grains of sand
The deafening silence is killing my ears

Am I crazy or worse, obsessed?
Piece by piece, things start to appear
And other things, well, they disappear
After a while, I leave the room
I question for a second
Did I make you up to replace my gloom?

Safiya Marbin (11)
Townley Grammar School For Girls, Bexleyheath

The Beautiful Truth

Amongst a world filled with deception,
Deception about fashion and beauty,
Deception about wealth and fame,
There lies a truth.

A truth about a girl,
A girl who lived in her truth,
Not ashamed to show who she really is,
A girl surrounded by a million truths.

Only expressing her natural self,
Not caring about what others thought of her,
Living in a carefree life,
With no pressure to look good for others.

The girl who only cared about her family,
The girl who inspired others to be who they are,
The only two things she cared about,
This was her beautiful truth.

Asmitha Cathiskanthan (12)
Townley Grammar School For Girls, Bexleyheath

Unheard Voices

Everywhere she goes,
All she hears are the unheard voices that follow,
All she sees are the stares, the glances, the looks,
Because all she is known as is that silenced black girl.
Struggling to find her identity,
Locked up in a cage of calamity,
Because all that she is, is that silenced black girl.
No one to call,
No one to visit when she is in a bore,
Because all that she is is that silenced black girl.
The truth is,
It was me,
That silenced black girl,
But no longer,
I am now the free black girl,
'That has been freed from the chains of'
'Silence'

Momore Sina-Atanda (12)
Townley Grammar School For Girls, Bexleyheath

Welcome To My Paradise

I feel the wind in my hair
And the sun on my cheeks
Come on!
Welcome to my paradise
Where I am free forever, free from fear
Come on!
Welcome to my paradise
Where no one is judged by their looks or their roots
Come on!
Welcome to my paradise
We all deserve to be here, we all deserve to live
Come on!
Welcome to my paradise
Be you, be real
Come on!
Welcome to my paradise.

Joanna Elegbede (11)
Townley Grammar School For Girls, Bexleyheath

Story

When you see a story what do you see?
A story between you and me,
a page.
No,
a story,
a story between you and me,
do you still see a page?
Yes,
really,
now let's talk about what I see,
I see a chapter waiting to be opened and seen,
a chapter to bring me my destiny,
my destiny, standing right in front of me.

Emilie King (11)
Townley Grammar School For Girls, Bexleyheath

The Beautiful Truth

A beautiful truth,
That reveals its face.
One sentimental thought,
Just so hard to erase.
Maybe something I remember,
Probably from my past.
Or a memory,
Could be the first or the last...

Anayah Springer (12)
Townley Grammar School For Girls, Bexleyheath

So What If You Can't Do Anything?

Even if you are full of fear
Even if you are full of unknowns about the future
Even there is nobody waiting for you at the end and supporting you
So, this is the reason why you must love and accept all of yourself
So, this is the reason why the world is sincere and kind and ready to hug you
There's nothing to be concerned about
Because miracles are hidden in your destiny
It is within reach, it is waiting for you
Just take your steps gently
Only then do you have a chance to find the cheers of victory.

Step by step, slowly and seriously
But on this trip, you will have an enemy
His name is your fear
All you need to do is disappear those eyes which filled with tears
You don't have to be afraid to duel with yourself
Because he is always denying and laughing
Because you know yourself better than he does.
You don't have to fight, you don't have to debate
Just stand there, stare at him and tell him what you anticipate
Comfort him quietly because he is a part of your bravery

The Beautiful Truth - Echoes Of Expression

Escape from bondage, pursue your freedom
Standing up to the gnarled promontory
Catharsis your despairs and sullenness to the sea.

If you want to retain a snowflake, it will melt faster in the palm of your hand
The only precious piece of white snow in the desert disappears in the warm hands
Maybe it's a wonderful destination, but why not let it sleep in the gravel?
But you have forgotten, there is no snow in the desert
It is your illusion, your desire for beauty
What you have seen, maybe is a raindrop or a gravel
But don't be disappointed; at least he taught you how to recognise yourself
Snowflakes are your hope, desert is your plight
Never be disquieted, steadily pursue your snowflakes
It may be as small, as subtle or as light as nothing
But as long as you try your best, nothing is impossible.

So what if you can't do anything?
That's just because the world hasn't discovered you yet
Have a leisurely pace
Because freedom means you don't have to do anything you don't want to do
Instead of doing whatever you want
Since you are not ready yet, take a break first
Because you were not born for comparison but for enjoyment

There is nothing to be concerned about
Even if you are full of unwillingness
Even if you are full of reluctance to let go of the past
Even if there is no one out there to lead you and encourage you.

Loneliness cries 'like a wounded wolf'
Which is not only the externalisation of its own pain
But of course, also includes the outpouring of sincere hope
Intimate your grin
A slightly raised smile contains enthusiasm, cheerful and passionate
The sunray is doffing out the sinfulness and murkiness
Life is like late spring grass, your observation is a novel
Time is novelist, years are its scribble and longhand
The wind is the sleepless bird, memory is the alluring and beautiful reflection
And you are your perfect self, unrestrained and full of vitality and hope.

Being yourself is always the best option
But be kind no matter what
This is the truth of the world.

Emma Wang (12)
Tudor Hall School, Banbury

I'll Rise

Inspired by 'And Still I Rise' by Maya Angelou

You may treat me like your slave
With your filthy reckless words
And your unacceptable lies
But still like a balloon, I rise.

You may step on me with your moves
You may skip me in the register
You may hit me with your belt
But still like the moon, I rise.

You may embarrass me every day
You may make me cry
You may tell people stuff about me
But still like the sun, I rise.

You may laugh at me (I don't care)
You may pinch me in the arm
You may talk behind my back
But still like a rocket, I rise.

Olivia Ormazabal (10)
Tudor Hall School, Banbury

Utopia Disguise

What hides under the surface,
You will never know,
Because the things I feel inside,
I will never show.

However,
Today is a different day,
And I will let you in
To the complicated mess
That lives beneath my skin.

I'm not all smiles and sunshine,
I'm not all warm, sweet glow,
And if you're the one that did this,
Love, I'll never show.

I may not ever meet you,
But don't you try to be
A better family than I have right now,
Because you couldn't look after me.

I know it's not your fault,
But partly you are to blame,
Because you're the reason why
I hate even my own name.

But enough about you,
More about me,

I would prefer not to delve
Into the depths of my family tree.

You know me as the quiet one,
And also never blue,
If that's what you're perceiving,
I've done well at lying to you.

Maisie Gross (12)
Tudor Hall School, Banbury

YOUNG WRITERS INFORMATION

We hope you have enjoyed reading this book – and that you will continue to in the coming years.

If you're the parent or family member of an enthusiastic poet or story writer, do visit our website **www.youngwriters.co.uk/subscribe** and sign up to receive news, competitions, writing challenges and tips, activities and much, much more! There's lots to keep budding writers motivated!

If you would like to order further copies of this book, or any of our other titles, then please give us a call or order via your online account.

Young Writers
Remus House
Coltsfoot Drive
Peterborough
PE2 9BF
(01733) 890066
info@youngwriters.co.uk

Join in the conversation!
Tips, news, giveaways and much more!

 YoungWritersUK   YoungWritersCW

 youngwriterscw   youngwriterscw